Escape to the Jungle

Escape to the Jungle

. . . and 31 other outstanding missionary stories

Compiled by Charles J. Guth
Edited by Marjory Koop
Illustrations and design: Charles J. Guth
Cover design: James Loates
Cover photo: Four by Five

An SIM publication

Escape to the Jungle

By SIM International

Printed in the United States of America

First Sonlight Curriculum, Ltd. Edition, 2001

For a catalog of Sonlight Curriculum materials for the home school, write:

SONLIGHT CURRICULUM, LTD.
8042 S. Grant Way
Littleton, CO 80122-2705
USA

Or e-mail: catalog@sonlight.com

These articles originally appeared in Africa Now (now SIM NOW), official publication of SIM. All unsigned articles were written by Kerry E. Lovering.

Contents

(Date of original publication in *Africa Now* follows title)

Escape to the jungle

To see soft-spoken Margaret Hayes going about her duties in a hospital on the edge of the Sahara wouldn't give you a clue that a few years ago her name was blazoned around the world as a missionary heroine.

Margaret disagreed with that when she came out of the Congo forests into world prominence in 1965, miraculously alive after having been presumed martyred. She still disagrees. She's not a heroine, she will tell you. She's simply a nurse, committed to obeying Christ's command to take the gospel to all people.

That commitment took Margaret first of all to Belgian Congo to work with Unevangelized Fields Mission. It also led to experiences that for many people would have written off further missionary involvement.

The first came in 1960, when the nation gained independence, under the name Zaire. Anti-white feelings were so intense that Margaret and her fellow missionaries had to be evacuated.

When that blew over, she returned, only to see the

Simba ("lion") rebellion burst into all-out carnage in 1964. Trapped at a village called Bopepe, where she ran a bush dispensary and a 12-bed hospital, Margaret was taken captive and marched 15 miles to another village, Banalia, where the Simbas were assembling white hostages.

In her book *Missing — Believed Killed* (Hodder and Stoughton), she recalled the ordeal that followed — 18 days of abuse and privation, terminated for her by an abrupt and unexplained order to return to Bopepe and resume her medical work.

The day after she left Banalia, government troops wrested the city of Stanleyville from the Simbas and freed some 1200 white hostages. In the fray, 37 of them were killed, including Dr. Paul Carlson and UFM missionary Hector McMillan.

The vengeful Simbas at Banalia retaliated the very next day by massacring all their white prisoners and dumping their bodies into the river, never to be recovered. The toll included 14 UFM missionaries and their six young children. When word of the slaughter reached the outside world, Margaret was listed as one of the martyrs. Only the Simbas knew that she was alive.

The word was soon out that they wanted her, too. Christian friends hid her in the forest for three weeks, while the Simbas tried to hunt her down. During those weeks Margaret had time to think. She concluded that for some reason known only to Him, God had spared her because He had more work for her to do.

"Then and there," she wrote, "in the solitude of the African jungle, with only the insects and trees as my witnesses, I rededicated my life afresh to the Lord, to go or stay, to die or live, in His service. This conviction has never left me."

It also dawned upon her that, being reported dead, no one at home would be praying for her. Appalled, she asked God to burden someone, daily, to intercede for her in prayer.

The fourth week was a nightmare. As the search intensified, she was compelled to move constantly, soaked by heavy rains, exhausted, legs swollen from infected insect bites. When she learned that every house in Bopepe had been burned to the ground and two villagers killed, she would not let her friends hide her any longer. She wrote a farewell note for her parents, walked painfully out of the forest, and surrendered.

To her surprise, the Simbas did not kill her. Instead, they made her their prisoner nurse, and for five long months compelled her to live among them as they went about their murderous business.

As the rebellion wound down, her captors went on a final rampage. They took over a Catholic convent and tortured and hacked to death 31 priests. One Simba severed a leg from one of the victims and made each of the nuns, and Margaret, hold it, in turn, while he warned them of their own impending fate.

Margaret's deliverance a month later by mercenary troops put her on the front pages of the world's press. "Innumerable emotions" filled her heart on her return home. Safe! It seemed unbelievable.

It seemed even more unbelievable to many people when, two years later, Margaret packed her goods and prepared to resume her work in Zaire. To Margaret it was not a remarkable decision. "The command to go has not yet been revoked," she explained.

On the eve of her departure, however, violence erupted again, right in the place to which she was going. Undismayed, she cast about for some other needy place, and found her way to the SIM hospital at Galmi, Niger Republic, on the edge of the Sahara.

A year later, with calm restored in Zaire, she resumed her work there, in the same setting which had held so much agony for her previously. She served for two full years before the care of her elderly mother required her return to England.

Her mother home in glory, Margaret returned to Galmi Hospital on the edge of the Sahara. A heroine? That depends on your definition. Brave? No question. But, most important, Margaret is committed. She made a promise to God, and she hasn't forgotten it.

Rain!

by Gordon Creighton

I suppose it was the visit of the local governor that finally made us call a day of prayer for rain.

The water situation was bad — not a drop of rain for six months. The streams that run from the edge of the great Rift Valley down into the lowlands had been drying up one by one.

Opportunists with farm tractors or small trucks had been dipping water from the streams that were still running, and selling it. This met the needs of those who could pay for it, at high prices, but the poorer people had to drink whatever they could find. Children began to die from disease picked up by drinking dirty water.

As the streams dried up, more and more people came to draw water from the small creek that supplies our work here at Shashemane, Ethiopia. We have the leprosarium, the hospital, the farm, the elementary school, the clinic, and the Bible school, as well as our missionary homes and Ethiopian staff homes. The meager water supply just wasn't enough for everything.

The governor had come to investigate charges that we were taking all the water from the creek, and letting none flow beyond our property. I led the group down to the little dam, to show how the trickle of water was divided, some for us, and the rest continuing downstream.

The governor was satisfied, but the incident caused us to realize that trouble could come, and perhaps we would have to cut back even further on our supply.

Two days later, we called a day of prayer for rain. There aren't a lot of believers in our area, but Christians are well known here because most of the people are Muslims. These Muslims are staunch in their beliefs, although there is a good deal of animism mixed into their religion.

To pray for rain was a real exercise of faith. We knew that pioneer missionaries had done it on occasion, but somehow it seemed different for us to do it! It was quickly known throughout the whole area what we were going to do. Some people mocked us. "We Muslims have been praying for rain for over a month," they said. "We've taken up collections all over the country to pay the rain-makers. The women have offered sacrifices at the rivers. They cried and cut themselves, pleading with the spirits. We'll see what *your* prayers will do!"

On Wednesday we closed everything on the station that

we could, and gathered in the church at 6 a.m. We prayed all day, and left the church at 10 p.m. The sky was clear and beautiful.

"Surely the Lord will honor His name and send rain," I thought, but my heart was full of doubt as I saw that starlit sky.

Next day we put our faith to work and got out our planting equipment. We plant about 600 acres of corn each year, plus 100 acres or more of potatoes, as well as other crops. That day we put everything in order for planting, while neighbors leaned on our fences, watching.

As the day wore on, clouds began to form, and my heart beat faster as the first promising drops fell in the evening.

During the night we had a light rain, but in the morning the earth was still as dry as ever. I decided to run the corn planter myself that day, and started off in the dust. By afternoon the clouds had gathered once again, and at 4 o'clock the rain came. I ended up happily drenched!

On Friday, more rain came, and from then on we had the usual showers every day.

On Sunday there was much praise to God in church. Six Muslim students stood and accepted Christ, convinced of God's power.

I don't know how many others have professed faith because of the rain, but there have been many. Word comes in from here and there that people have seen God answer the Christians' prayer, and want to trust Him.

Most, of course, continue as before. After the rains had started, some of the Christians were talking with a farmer. "What are you wearing those for?" they asked him, pointing to the beads around his neck and the amulets on his arms.

"Oh," he replied, "I have to. The Christians, they pray

and God gives to them, but me, I have to wear these things."

My prayer is that these people will accept God's greatest gift, Jesus Christ, the Living Water.

Assignment: Gola!

Hardly anyone remembers that shrewd old trader now. A Muslim of the Mandingo tribe, he showed up in the marketplaces of the Gola people about 15 years ago, using an ingenious little scheme to attract business.

On his stall he kept a radio, and in his head the daily schedule of Gola language programs from SIM's gospel radio station ELWA. At the right time he switched the radio on to full volume. As singing and preaching in their own language blasted through the markets, potential customers flocked to see what it was all about.

The trader didn't realize it, but he was introducing more than his wares. Other radio users also caught on, and ELWA's broadcasts soon became regular fare throughout the area. When the trader moved on, the gospel remained.

The Gola people live about 100 miles in the interior of Liberia. They are about 65,000 strong, most of them farmers, and most of them spirit-worshipers. Islam is there, too, not in strength, but with more converts now than there used to be. There has been some gospel influence where the Golas border on other tribes, but no significant penetration.

ELWA's broadcasts, however, took the gospel to every corner of Gola country every day of the week. The response was remarkable, although largely unknown to

ELWA at the time. Little groups of believers began to spring up here and there throughout the tribe.

These new Christians soon found, though, that daily radio programs did not provide them with all the spiritual nurture they needed. They wanted to learn more. Eventually the believers at a place called Gondatown got together and sent a messenger to the coast. They wanted ELWA to send them a missionary.

SIM's Arn Lueders was chosen to explore the situation. When he reached Gondatown he was warmly welcomed, and put up for the night by the government diamond commissioner (Liberia has many small diamond mining operations), a kindly Liberian of Anglican background, named James B. Ware.

Arn's meeting with the believers was unforgettable. He couldn't promise them a missionary, he explained, but he counseled them and encouraged them to form themselves into a local church. Before he left, they held their first baptismal service, with 70 believers following Christ in the waters of baptism.

After Arn left, the believers put up a building where they met for worship and prayer. But they had no trained pastor. They placed a radio on the clay pulpit and let it preach to them.

Things went well for a while, but no missionary came. ELWA wasn't able to start church planting at that time, and other missions likewise were fully committed.

The "hidden church" of Gondatown started to decline.

Tribal pressures were too much for some. They went back to animistic practices, or converted to Islam. The band of 70 slowly shrank. Other little congregations struggled, too.

But they were God's people and He didn't forget them. They still had the radio programs, and there were a few who could read the Bible. What they lacked was shepherds who could lead them and teach them.

God had one such man ready in the person of James Varney, a Liberian employee at ELWA. The Gola Christians became a special concern to him. He didn't consider himself a preacher, but whenever he could, he would travel into Gola country as far as the bus route went and walk out from there to pray and share with little groups.

So the infant church stayed alive. It didn't flourish, but it lived.

While it was struggling, tumultuous events were happening in Ethiopia, on the other side of the continent. SIM missionaries who could not continue their work there because of the revolution were seeking God's guidance regarding other places of service.

Ten years after Arn Lueders's visit, an SIM survey team that included three missionaries from Ethiopia found its way back to Gondatown.

One of the three was Malcolm Hunter, who tells how the team was drawn almost irresistibly past other tribes. "We looked for a place to spend the night," he related, "and asked for beds at an old diamond mining camp on the border of Gola country. We were given a cordial welcome by the government agent, a gracious, elderly man, who quietly explained that he had given hospitality to Arn Lueders 10 years ago in Gondatown! His name was James B. Ware.

"As we met for prayer, Mr. Ware joined us, pleading that the light of the gospel might soon shine among the Gola people, who had been waiting so long. We were deeply moved."

At Gondatown next morning they found that only 10 of the original 70 still called themselves Christians. One wall of the church building had collapsed, and the benches were rotting away.

"They told us that for the first while nearly the whole village had come to the church," Malcolm recalled. "In fact, they came from other villages miles away to see what church was all about. But they had no relevant Bible teaching, and that embryonic movement toward Christ withered away. It was a classic example of just how far a church can grow on evangelistic preaching alone, with no one to lead them into Bible truths."

Les Unruh was also from Ethiopia. "That survey trip through Gola country challenged my heart," he said. "One man sat there and said, 'You know, we don't want to be Muslims. We want to be Christians. But nobody has come to teach us.'

"I determined in my heart that I would do what I could. Back at ELWA, I told SIM administration that if they, too, felt this was God's guidance, I was willing to go to the Golas."

That was in February 1978. On June 20, an SIM delegation led by a beaming Les accepted title to 15 acres of land at Tahn, not far from Gondatown, for the establishment of a mission base.

District dignitaries and chiefs gathered for the festive occasion. The local commissioner welcomed SIM to Tahn, and in keeping with tribal tradition presented Les with a white chicken, symbol of friendship.

Les responded for the Mission with other traditional gifts. First was a white cloth, speaking of purity. "My heart is pure toward you," he explained. "The Word of God also tells us that God sent His Son to purify our hearts. Through Him, though our sins be as scarlet, they can be as white as snow."

Next was silver as a token of sincerity, then a goat,

which was cooked for the meal. "Traditionally this gift would be tobacco," Les explained. "I have replaced it with a goat because it, too, speaks of fellowship, which we have enjoyed as we've eaten together." The fourth gift was also a substitute — Coca-Cola instead of gin! The commissioner accepted it cheerfully. "We will always work together," he said, "so we thank you very much."

Others also expressed their pleasure. "We were in darkness at times," one town chief said, "but we are in the light with your coming to us."

Les couldn't build then because the rainy season was beginning. In Liberia that means three months of being washed away (Monrovia's average rainfall for July is 27.4 inches; last July it had 19 inches in two days). The Mission rented a house in Tahn so Les and Verla could move in, lay plans, and get started on the language. It was an exciting time, highlighted by seeing their landlord, a respected Justice of the Peace, make a commitment to Christ.

Early this year.Les finished building the Mission house and moved his family in. "It's bush work all over again," he explains. "Entering a new area like this you have to earn the right to share Jesus Christ. You have to live with these people and let them see your Christian life, and then they'll listen to what you have to say."

One of Les's top priorities is to strengthen leadership among the struggling Christian community. "There are 'pastors' here who are barely able to read," he says. "Some have no education, some have only first, second, or third grade. They preach only what they hear on the radio. But if we can train these men, and add some young blood, the church here will soon be restablished."

His immediate tool for that is a home study program. Theological Education by Extension (TEE) enables individuals to study the Bible at home, using instruction materials that are checked by an instructor at regular intervals. For those with limited reading ability, cassette tapes provide the lessons.

"We want to expand that ministry, and begin a Bible school," Les explains. "I want to see these pastors come to the place that when I leave Gola country I can go with the assurance that the church is here to stay. That's why I'm investing myself in the lives of these men."

Les is appealing for more missionaries. "There's a real sense of excitement to see what God is going to do next. Something is waiting to happen here, and we need more workers because right now the Gola people are ready to respond. They tell me they don't want to be Muslims, but they've nobody to lead them in the Christian way. We need a crew of new missionaries who are willing to dig in here and do just that."

"It is God's time," Mr. Ware told Les. "Gola is going to open up, you'll see!" When it does, it will become a stepping-stone into other tribes — *but only if there are messengers of the gospel to pioneer them.*

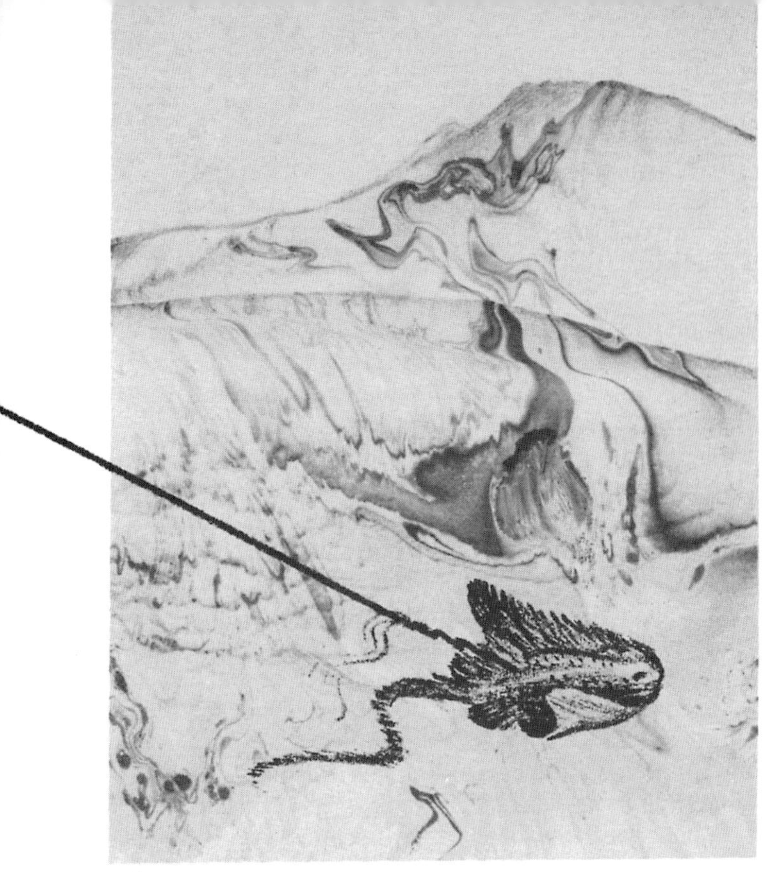

Our prayer by the Red Sea

by Norene Bond

It happened on the shore of the Red Sea in northern Ethiopia. We had just pitched camp on the beautiful white sand, and Bruce and the three boys had gone off to spear some fish for supper.

Or so they thought.

This was a very special adventure for our family. We had traveled three days from our SIM station to visit this exotic place. Fancy *us* being on the shore of the Red Sea!

It took only a few minutes to pile out of the car and put our camp in order. The tide was receding, leaving shallow pools and swirling eddies, and the prospect of spearing a nice big fish was good. So the hunters hurried off while Becky and I got out the frying pan.

"There's a big one!" someone shouted, and four figures raced toward a shallow place, where something huge was churning around in an attempt to find deeper water.

"Come on, boys!" shouted an excited Bruce. "Watch your father spear supper!" He hefted the beautifully balanced shaft and let it fly with a mighty swing. There was a rewarding thud as the point hit home. "Got him!" Bruce exulted. But before it could be captured, the intended victim flapped furiously over a sand bar and began its escape.

"It's a stingray!" the boys shouted in dismay. "And he's taking the spear with him!"

A chagrined foursome watched helplessly as the great, flat body slowly headed out to sea, the spear submerging like the periscope of a submarine. "Oh, well," one of the boys said, "we wanted a *real* fish anyway, not a stingray."

"But the spear!" another voice groaned. "It's not ours, you know!"

Missionary friends had urged the spear on us, insisting that we borrow it for our expedition. It was a beautiful, handmade instrument, quite expensive, and almost impossible to replace. We had accepted the offer hesitantly. We didn't know how we could fit such a long object into the car, and we didn't want it to get broken.

Now the worst had happened.

As we lay in our sleeping bags on the sand that night—

after a supper of beans — we had our evening prayers together. Before we finished, Becky's little voice broke the stillness. "Daddy, can't we ask God to give us back our spear?"

We have always taught our children that God answers prayer. Now Becky was putting us to the test — over a spear and a stingray, of all things. Our faith was rather weak, but we agreed. We asked the Lord for the spear back, and soon dropped off to sleep.

Early next morning, Bruce crept out of his sleeping bag and prowled along the beach, half hoping that the spear had been washed ashore during the night. It hadn't.

Simple family prayers followed breakfast, during which Becky again reminded us to pray about our loss. A couple of hours later we all went swimming in the warm, tropical waters. All but Bruce, that is, who elected to keep an eye on the camp. Anyway, the loss of the spear had taken the edge off his enthusiasm for water sports.

Suddenly a cry went up: "Stingray! Dad! A stingray!"

Bruce wasn't impressed. He'd seen enough stingrays for one holiday.

The cry persisted: "Dad! It's the one with the spear!"

That was different. Bruce leaped into action. Quickly, he dug out a large fishhook and tied it to the end of a long pole. He waded into the water, hardly believing his eyes. It had been 16 long hours since that thing had swum away, with the whole Red Sea to disappear into. But here it was, back again, within half a mile of where it had left.

Another reason to marvel was that it stayed close to shore, gliding around gracefully within Bruce's reach, while he angled for it. After a few attempts, Bruce managed to slip the hook around the shaft, and felt the point dig into the wood. A firm tug released the spear, and the stingray sped out to sea.

All we could think of was how God had made the iron ax head swim in the Jordan River for Elisha. Now God had done practically the same thing for us, making iron swim right out of the Red Sea and into our hands.

Becky, of course, was delighted. "Daddy," she said triumphantly, "God does answer prayer, doesn't He?"

The testing of Peter Pan

by Leona Choy, Ambassadors for Christ

Peter slumped in his wheelchair on the hospital sun porch. "Is God mocking me?" he fretted. "How could He lead me through years of medical school, and then let me be stricken with cavitary tuberculosis two weeks before graduation?"

Disillusionment engulfed him. "It isn't for myself I've worked day and night to become a surgeon," his heart cried out. "It was for *you,* God! I want to spread the gospel in foreign lands!"

Despite his outburst, Peter Pan knew in his heart that God had His hand upon him. During the past month in the isolation ward he had had time to think long and hard about the way God had led him.

Peter was born in Luichow, China. When he was five, his family fled from the Communists to Hong Kong. Seven years later, in 1956, they moved to California. In those first 11 years of his life, Peter had scant exposure to Christianity, and knew nothing of salvation.

But during high school, God found him. A Chinese friend invited him to a Christian meeting, and there he made his decision for Christ.

University, however, became a spiritual wilderness. He switched his major from engineering to physics to chemistry, restless, not knowing how to find God's will. "Where is that abundant life Christ promised?" he wondered.

He found the answer at a Chinese for Christ summer conference. The Holy Spirit applied Romans 12:1 and 2 to his heart: "I beseech you therefore, brethren, by the mercies of God, that ye present your bodies a living sacrifice, holy, acceptable unto God, which is your reasonable service.

"And be not conformed to this world; but be ye transformed by the renewing of your mind, that ye may prove what is that good, and acceptable, and perfect, will of God." And Peter Pan gave himself to the Lord without reservation. Feeling a compulsion to medical missions, he applied to the University of Cincinnati College of Medicine, and was accepted.

Although he reveled in his high calling, he kept his nose in his books the first two years at the expense of spiritual growth. Then came a turning point — a summer at Manorom Christian Hospital in Thailand, with Overseas Missionary Fellowship. The experience turned his missionary zeal into a steady flame, impelling him through the remaining grueling years of study.

Then came the cough and the fever, and the eve of his graduation found him alone on the hospital sun porch, his dreams and plans dashed upon the rocks of illness.

Peter weathered the storm, however, by turning once again to the Lord of his life. During the long months of recuperation, he dug diligently into the Word of God. "It turned out to be the most fruitful year of my spiritual growth," he said later.

Recovery was slow. After a year, Peter's X-rays still showed incomplete healing. He remembered dragging his feet as he left the lab one day, hearing the surgeon's statement: "You must have surgery to remove the affected lung."

Peter knew that this was a hazardous operation. It would probably shelve forever his plans to be a missionary. As he pondered his situation, he felt constrained to delay surgery. After a week of prayer, God gave him peace about the decision. He told the surgeon: "No." With his wife, Sylvia, he returned to the warmer climate of California.

Sylvia. God had His hand upon her life, too. She was born in Hong Kong, into an upright but non-Christian home where religion was rarely mentioned. "I thought religion was for old folks," she had told Peter. That was before she went to U.S.A., to study at the University of Cincinnati.

There, away from home, facing language difficulties and the pressure of study, the need for God began to rise within her. When she was invited by Chinese Christians to a home Bible study, she accepted. There she was exposed to God's love and learned the plan of salvation. Her longing for peace soon prevailed. She accepted Christ, and dedicated herself to serve Him.

And she met Peter.

In Los Angeles, Peter and Sylvia looked to God for guidance. "Strangely, the Lord seemed to impress me to keep on with my medical training," Peter recalled. "I started my internship — a year late — pushing myself to near exhaustion, and resigned to being a TB cripple."

Supposing the door to missions permanently closed, he changed from a surgical residency to one in anesthesia. "But the thought of missions was ever with me," Peter said, "even though I regularly complained how TB had ruined my life."

He will never forget the day in 1975 when, after his usual lament, the doctor said: "Stop kidding yourself. There's no reason why you can't go to the mission field. Your treatment has been successful!"

Overjoyed, he wrote to SIM. Did they need an anesthesiologist? They did — and the rest is a matter of record. Dr. Peter Pan is presently on staff at Egbe Hospital, Nigeria.

"Our Lord has been with us always, and we thank Him for giving us sufficient grace to go though all our difficulties," Peter wrote recently. "It is exciting to be here, though we admit it was not easy. There are many adjustments to make, and a lot of new things to learn. We wait before the Lord for the years ahead, and praise Him for whatever He is going to do with us here."

"Hallelujah is the same in any language!"

Tom Archibald, Scottish, grizzled, blue eyes twinkling, stood respectfully as Nigeria's head of state mounted the school platform. "A handsome lad," thought Tom approvingly, as the uniformed figure took the place of honor.

Lad? General Yakubu Gowon, military chief of staff, head of Africa's most populous nation?

To Tom Archibald, yes. At 76 years of age, Tom was nearly old enough to be the General's grandfather. Just yesterday, December 10, 1971, there had been a great celebration marking Tom and Grace Archibald's 50 years of service in Nigeria. Tom and his bride had arrived from Scotland in 1921, thirteen years before Yakubu Gowon had been born.

Yesterday Tom had relived those years. Today the memories crowded in again. Just a few minutes ago, on the way to the school, he and Grace had passed the great tree, ancient landmark of Kagoro. To the children of the town it was a place to play. It hadn't always been.

The Kagoros had been demon worshipers, headhunters who demanded a human trophy from every prospective bridegroom. When Tom built the two-room mud brick house and moved Grace and the baby into it, the tree was sacred to the demons. More than once Tom had ignored the blood offerings smeared on its massive trunk and reached deep into its hollow place to rescue a baby left there to die.

That was in 1927. Before then, British authorities had refused permission for white peole to live in Kagoro. "It's not safe," they said. When Tom and Grace and three Nigerian Christian families moved to Kagoro from Kwoi, 40 miles away, they were the first ones to carry the gospel light into that "great darkness."

Those were the words that Chief Gwamna Nwaya had used yesterday. "Our town was in great darkness," he said. "We had no knowledge of the Word of God, or of reading or writing. Yet these good friends loved and embraced us, and what changes have been wrought!"

Yes, God had changed many lives at Kagoro. Chief Gwamna was one example. He sat on the platform, quiet, dignified, wearing the Order of the British Empire medal, bestowed upon him by Queen Elizabeth II. Gwamna was not only Chief of Kagoro and president of a federation of chiefs who were responsible for nearly half-a-million people, but also a capable preacher. "Righteousness exalteth a nation . . . . " "The entrance of thy word giveth light . . . . " How often Tom had heard him use these favorite texts.

Tom looked upon Gwamna almost as a son. When Tom arrived at Kagoro, Gwamna was a fatherless nine-year-old. Within a year, Tom had led him to the Lord. Tom taught him the Bible, Grace taught him to cook. Later they sent him off to train as a teacher. As the years passed, he became scribe to the chief, then succeeded him in office.

"He's a good lad, too," Tom mused. Not very long ago Tom had dropped into Gwamna's house unexpectedly. It was nearly noon, and he did not intend to stay. But as they chatted, the chief quietly excused himself and left the room. He returned carrying a tray laden with tea and toast and eggs. "I haven't forgotten how to fry your eggs, you know," he grinned. He had prepared the lunch himself.

Quite a change from the early days, Tom remembered. The Kagoros had been hostile at first, refusing even to sell them food. But they did need medical help, and gradually Grace's skill and kindness drew increasing numbers to the little house each day. Tom soon began using his reputation for extracting teeth as a means of filling the larder. He charged one chicken per tooth, and kept them supplied with eggs and meat.

The Archibalds were too friendly to be rejected for long. Tom played with the children as he visited and preached, and soon became known as Dachip, "the one who amuses." Grace they named Dariya, meaning "laughter."

Conversions began slowly, one here, one there. At first the new Christians received strong opposition from their people, especially from the juju men, leaders of demon worship. On one occasion the juju leaders secretly decided to sacrifice a young Christian named Garba as a warning to the tribe. Garba's father learned of the plot, and warned Garba, expecting him to flee. He didn't. Garba stood firm, declaring Christ's power to protect him. The juju men backed down. They beat two other Christians to save face, but the power of juju was never again strong.

From Kagoro, Tom and the Kwoi Christians moved out to the surrounding areas. "He always had time to sit by our fires and talk to us," the old recalled. "He never refused anything we offered him. He walked from village to village, sitting with us, eating the food we ate, sleeping where we slept, and always telling us of Jesus Christ."

One of Tom's close companions during those days was Toro. "Toro would have liked to be here," thought Tom, glancing around the crowded auditorium. But Toro was in heaven. Tom remembered the night Toro died. He had been ill for some time. That evening he called his family together and counseled them once more to stay close to the Lord. Then he began to pray. As he prayed his voice became weaker and weaker. He whispered to his son, "The light hurts my eyes."

The boy turned the tiny lamp down until the room was almost in darkness. "You are turning it up!" exclaimed Toro. "The brightness is more than I can stand!" And Toro entered glory.

Experiences like that more than repaid Tom and Grace for 50 years of service. Never would Tom forget the words of one Kagoro Christian: "I thank you for two things," he said. "You have taken away the fear which I had while living; and the fear which I would have had while dying."

Tom's memory flew back to one of the first baptisms. It was in 1932, just five years since they had reached Kagoro. Sixteen men and six women had been accepted. Tom had felt like shouting, "Hallelujah!" as soon as the service began. By the time the last one came out of the water, he couldn't hold it any longer. "Hallelujah is the same in any language," he explained to his supporters at home, "so I started up the Hallelujah Chorus. Once wasn't enough; we sang it twice. I don't know how it sounded to the pagans, but to me it sounded heavenly!"

It had sounded heavenly to Bagaiya, too. Bagaiya was pastor of the Kagoro church. He had grown up with Gwamna, and had been sent to school with him by the Archibalds. He knew all the early converts, and had seen the church grow from its very beginning. He had seen the first church building, which seated 125, almost bursting at the seams within seven years of the Archibalds' arrival. Tom called a meeting. The congregation enthusiastically decided to build one that would hold 500. "When shall we start?" Tom had asked. "Tomorrow!" came the answer. On the spot they divided into work groups, chose leaders, and assigned each crew one day of the week for labor.

At the dedication of the new building, there were 400 present. They sang "Holy, Holy, Holy!" and Tom thought his heart would burst. That same afternoon they started the first annual Bible Conference.

On the tenth anniversary, they took a special offering. It came to about $23. The elders asked Tom to send some of it to East Africa, to the SIM missionaries who were just opening new territory in the Anglo-Egyptian Sudan [now called Sudan Republic]. They wanted a share in reaching the unreached Nilotic people with the gospel.

And there was the church's 30th anniversary! What a gift the church had given Tom and Grace! Pastor Bagaiya had explained what they were going to do. They were going to win more people to Christ. "Next week has been set aside for prayer," he said. "The following two weeks will be for visitation and preaching. Then we will bring all the new converts here to the home of our beloved parents, the Archibalds."

When the day came, thousands of people flocked in to Kagoro. The peak of rejoicing came when the new believers stood and their number was given — over one thousand! The words of Bagaiya's closing prayer still rang in Tom's ears. "Our Father, we thank you very, very much. Give us wisdom as we tie these new converts on our backs and carry them in our hearts."

And carry them they had. There were believers in every town and village for miles around. There were churches and Sunday schools. There was the Bible School and the Secondary School. The headhunters of Kagoro had become followers of Christ.

Suddenly Tom heard his name. General Gowon was speaking. He was talking about "our respected missionaries, Reverend and Mrs. Archibald."

He had not been present at the Archibalds' anniversary celebrations yesterday, he explained, but it was his pleasure to thank them now for their service to the people of Nigeria. "May I congratulate Mr. Archibald," he said, "on his foresight in setting up this College, which is doing great service, not only to the people of this State, but to the whole of this nation. May God bless him and bless his work!"

Then, as the students clapped wildly, General Yakubu Gowon left the platform and made his way to where the

Archibalds sat. He took Grace's hand and shook it. He took Tom's hand and shook it. "Thank you," he said.

A few minutes later the assembly dismissed. Tom again stood respectfully as the official party departed. Then, grizzled, kindly, blue eyes twinkling, he took his wife's hand. "Come, Mother," he said, and led her to the door.

Together they made their way down the road, past the buildings, past the great old tree, toward the mud brick house and home.

What now, Mrs. Kirk?

Myrtle Kirk looks like someone out of a storybook. She is a sweet little lady, with silver hair and gentle smile. A widow, she lives alone in a neat little house surrounded by flowers and shrubs. Her door is open to young people. Her house is filled with music. She is mother, grandmother, friend, and counselor.

But she is more than just a storybook character. She is a hardy, practical, determined little woman who has spent 41 years in Nigeria as a missionary.

She has had her share of hardships; she has done a lot of living, and she has made the people of Nigeria the focus of her love and concern.

She is still in Nigeria, at Kagoro, in her little house with flowers. But not for much longer. Next spring Myrtle Kirk will retire. That means coming "home" to Canada. But after 41 years in Nigeria, is Canada really home?

"I have mixed feelings about that," she says. "If it weren't for the anticipation of living on the same continent as my children and grandchildren, I'd like to stay out here. If the government would let me, that is. And the Mission. But it doesn't work, really, to retire in Africa, so I'm happy to go back. Being with my family is the one thing I am looking forward to above all else."

It will take some adjusting, though. "I shall miss many

things," she explains. "The beautiful scenery here, the flowering trees, the frangipani, the flamboyants, the bougainvillias, the jacarandas, the wild orchid trees. And I shall miss my roses. They bloom all year here. I shall miss the tropical fruit that grows in my yard, the bananas, papayas, guavas, avocado pears, oranges, tangerines, grapefruit, and pineapple.

"And I shall miss the different sounds. They're so interesting. In the early morning you can hear the donkeys braying, the drumming down in the village, the doves cooing. You can hear the bells ringing at the school, and the students singing as they go on their way to school.

"But most of all I shall miss my students. I shall miss teaching them and all the discussions we have, and teaching them to sing. They love to sing! Ever since I've been at Kagoro — 18 years now — I've had full responsibility for the music. I've taught them piano and music and singing, and I've enjoyed it so much.

"I shall miss listening to their trials and troubles, and sharing their hopes for the future. I shall miss the teachers at the Bible College, Africans and missionaries alike. Most of my missionary friends my age have retired. The ones I have now are all much younger than I. They help to keep me young, so I'll miss them, too."

There are some things she won't miss, though, even when the cold Canadian winter settles in. "I shall not miss the very hot weather. The hot season this year seems to have been exceptionally long and trying. The harmattan, the fine dust that blows in off the Sahara, has been so thick you couldn't even see the hills, so close to our school. I shall not miss the long wet season, either. Day after day for weeks you do not go out the door without boots and umbrella. Miss the climate? No, not really. Miss the people? Oh, yes!"

Retirement will mean starting housekeeping all over again for Myrtle Kirk. She doesn't plan on taking household goods home, except for a few small items. "After 41 years out here, what is there worth taking back? I have a few things with sentimental value, but nothing worth transporting.

"Yes, I will have to start all over again. Apart from a tea set that I left in Canada, and a few pots and pans, I haven't anything. Where will I find the money to set up house again? Well, I've tried to put aside a little, which will be a help, but the Lord has so abundantly cared for me all these years, I'm sure I'll not lack anything I need."

Myrtle Kirk's confidence in God's provision shows through readily. She's trusted Him all her life, and found Him equal to all her needs. So she isn't worried about the high cost of living in Canada.

"I'll get the government pension for senior citizens," she says, "and SIM will supplement that, if necessary, to bring it up to the same amount as the Mission salary for the month. I shall have to ask the Mission for rent, though. SIM has a retirement fund, but it's only been going for a few years, and I really don't see how the Mission can provide for rent and other expenses. But whatever the Lord sends in will be enough. I believe He supplies all our needs, but not necessarily our wants.

It means that the Mission will still need some support for me, though, just as it does now. To help with rent, and pay medical bills, and things like that are expenses that continue even after retirement. And I think my friends who have been supporting me all these years would understand that, if it were explained to them. Some of my supporters are old age pensioners now, of course, but I believe they understand these things. I've trusted the Lord all these years, and I'm not looking to man to supply the needs. I believe the Lord will care for me in retirement."

Where will she live? At this stage, she doesn't know. "I'll likely stay with my daughter and son-in-law, until the Lord shows me definitely what He has for me to do. I still feel young enough and active enough to do something besides sitting in a rocking chair. I trust that I can get something to do, be somewhere where I can help. I want to keep busy in whatever the Lord has for me to do. I don't have many answers yet, but I don't have any apprehensions, either."

Retirement will bring many changes. Separation from Africa and her African friends will bring times of nostalgia. But Myrtle Kirk doesn't expect to be lonely. "I have friends scattered from one side of Canada to the other. I have a number of hobbies, and I enjoy reading and studying. And, of course, my music. No, I don't think I shall be lonely."

One question that many people ask her is: "Who will take your place in Nigeria?" She doesn't have an answer for that.

"I've enjoyed my work out here, and when I leave I don't know who'll take my place, but I have perfect peace of heart, knowing that I've been doing the Lord's will. The students keep asking: 'Who will teach us music when you leave?' and I don't know. We shall be getting Nigerian staff to teach my Bible classes, and Missions, and English, and Deeper Spiritual Life, but there's no one in sight for the music. I simply tell them: 'The Lord will provide.' "

So Myrtle Kirk will leave her house at Kagoro, and pack her few belongings, and come "home" to Canada and her family, confident that the Lord who has led her and met her needs for over 40 years will continue at her side.

"I consider it a great privilege to have had these years out here in Africa," she says. "I wouldn't have exchanged it for anything at home. To think that the Lord has seen fit not only to bring me out to Africa but to keep me all these years! So many missionaries labor under great difficulties, but the Lord has given me strength and health, and I want to praise Him right now for that. I want my life in the future to be used of Him, too. I don't want to be put away on the shelf. I am looking forward to retirement, and to whatever the Lord has for me."

And knowing that the Lord *does* have something in store for her is quite enough for Myrtle Kirk.

Mrs. Kirk came home in 1974, to retire in western Canada. In 1977 the leaders of the Evangelical Churches of West Africa (SIM-related) requested that she return for a special assignment. Myrtle spent a happy year back in Nigeria helping with the revision of the Hausa hymnbook.

Ambush!

In the black night of the Algerian mountain, big Jean Klopfenstein hugged the ground and prepared to die. Machine gun bullets spewed dirt into his face. The man behind Jean screamed. The guerrillas' ambush of the army patrol was complete. Jean knew he would not live through this one.

Jean was a Christian, but he had little to offer God. Sports and excitement had been his life. A great sadness swept over him as he committed himself to God.

As abruptly as it started, however, the terror ended. The soldiers retreated, leaving Jean for dead. He lay still for a time, then crept to the friend behind him. He was wounded, but still alive. Jean put his arms around him and stumbled with him to safety.

At the base, Jean learned that the platoon leader was missing. No one would attempt rescue. Jean headed back into the darkness alone, returning with the leader slung across his shoulders. He had been killed, just a few yards from where Jean had lain.

Jean tended his wounded companion until a rescue helicopter arrived at dawn. Then tension caught up with him. Lying on his bed, he sought solace in his Bible.

Reading 1 Chronicles 29:14, Jean was struck by David's statement that what he had given to God was only what God had first given to him. David was just giving things back again.

Jean saw a parallel. During the ambush, God had given him a new life. Jean hadn't expected deliverance, or prayed for it. Death was so certain that he had simply handed himself over to God. But here he was, very much alive. It was as though God had said: "Jean, here's a new life for you."

Jean decided he would give it back. From now on, he would make that life really count for Christ.

Jean had been born to missionary parents in French Guiana, where his father had worked among the convicts of Devil's Island. As a child, Jean trusted Christ for salvation. On their return to France shortly before World War II, the family's faith was tested severely. They were very poor, and Jean became so undernourished that the Red Cross sent him to Switzerland for rehabilitation. He remembered one occasion when there was, literally, no food in the house. His mother asked God to send them some. That very day, a relative brought them provisions from a farm. Jean never forgot that. As he grew up, Jean attended church regularly.

At 14, however, a realization of what sin really was kept him awake one night. Concerned about what would happen if he died, he woke his parents. They prayed with him, and from then on Jean had no doubt that he was saved.

But his interest in spiritual things waned. He grew tall and husky, and sports became his consuming interest.

At age 20 he was drafted. His size and strength made him an obvious choice for machine gunner, but Jean didn't like that. He refused. During graduation parade, however, he was ordered to hold the gun, to impress the inspecting officer. Jean's heart went to his mouth when the officer asked Jean how competent he was with his weapon. Risking discipline, Jean replied that he didn't know how to use it at all — he really wanted to be a medic. To Jean's surprise, the officer arranged a transfer.

When he was posted to Algeria during that country's fight for independence, he quickly gained respect for his medical skill. Soon he was cited for rescuing a badly wounded soldier and keeping him alive by consulting with a doctor on radio until a rescue helicopter arrived.

Jean didn't know it as he lay on his bed reading his Bible, but this deed of the night before was to earn him another citation. Later, he would be cited yet again by the Red Cross for his medical work in the village near the army camp.

Jean's commitment took definite shape during the weeks that followed. He would attend Bible school, he decided, and return to Africa as a missionary.

The day after his two-year military service ended, he was moved out of the fighting zone. Fighting had not ceased, though, and as they left, his group was ambushed. Seven of Jean's companions were killed. By the time he reached France, Jean was absolutely certain that God had spared his life for a reason.

At the Bible school in Geneva, Switzerland, Jean came into contact with SIM. He was impressed with two needs for French-speaking West Africa: nurses and teachers. After much prayer he went to the principal and told him of his decision to complete medical training as a nurse, and then serve with SIM.

Then he met Roselyne, also a student. Enamored though he was, Jean's commitment to Christ came first. Early in their friendship he explained that God had called him to SIM's Francophone Area. Roselyne brightened. She had been wondering how to tell Jean of *her* decision — to be a teacher in SIM Francophone.

After marriage, and Jean's graduation as a nurse, they applied to SIM. In 1963 they went to Niger, and "big Jean" later became director of SIM's Francophone Area — the countries of Niger, Upper Volta, and Benin.

Over the years Jean learned that the battle is spiritual, not military, but Jean still follows the well-learned principles of obedience and discipline. "God led me here," he says. "He has a reason."

Now there is a church in Dompagoland

from the letters of Roland Pickering

January 1951, Stratford, Ontario, Canada

Many missionary candidates find that before God definitely shows them their particular place of service, they themselves must take some initial steps of faith. In his wonderful vision of the Lord, Isaiah saw God in search of a volunteer. "Whom shall I send?" This messenger was not to be a victim of the irresistible divine command, but a volunteer. It is to this place in my own experience that I have come. Having heard the Lord's call for volunteer messengers, I have said with all my heart: "Here am I, send me."

July 1951, Stratford

The SIM Toronto Council accepted me. The West Africa Field Director sent a letter making it clear that the most suitable place would be French country, and advising a customary period of language study in France. August 8 I sail from Quebec City.

December 1951, France

The Field Council will soon be telling me the station that I will be going to in Dahomey [now called Benin]. Pray that the Lord will have His way in this matter, for I want to be in the place where I can serve best.

April 1952, Djougou, Dahomey

I expect to be stationed at Dompago, center of a farming district. The opportunity is very great. When our missionary Paul Clapp was in the area not long ago, he found many proofs of eagerness to hear the gospel. At one spot he used a mile-and-a-quarter road that Dompagos had built to their village seven years earlier, when they heard that a missionary was going to visit them. At another place, the chief ordered the village market to stop, and made everybody listen to the message.

In the face of such great openings you can understand why I ask for your earnest prayers. If from the very start we can move forward together, full of faith, surely we can look to see our request fulfilled.

September 1952, Dompago

Late in the afternoon of June 16 a new station opened here in Dahomey — Dompago. I remember that first day well. The people who had milled noisily around me since my arrival had drifted away to their huts to eat. The Jeep that had brought me had disappeared along the path.

I stood in front of my house [mud and thatch] looking toward the fading sun. Although I had been in Africa since April, this seemed somehow to be the first time I actually felt I was here, and here to stay.

A few steps to my right stood the little mud church, dark

and empty, a grass mat across the doorway to keep goats out. [This chapel was the result of work by an evangelist from the Methodists who had worked among the Dompagos previously. It is not clear whether there were any Christians there when Roland arrived.]

To the left the first walls of the village began. Behind them stretched a mass of little peaks, each one the roof of another tiny, smoky hut, someone's home. It was then that Africa began to settle in around me. There was no "civilization" to turn back to, no clean, airy mission house to flee to. I wasn't looking at slides any more!

Since then, the work has gone apace. There are now 10 young men in a baptismal class. They will be the first members of the church when they have demonstrated their new faith by consistent living. I have great hope for them.

Language study continues to be my first duty. It comes slowly, but will pay precious dividends one day.

June 1953, Dompago

Sometimes, as I am teaching my boys or young men, pressing upon them the claims of Christ, I will see a glimmer of light break across the earnest faces of two or three. One of them will say: "Let us pray that these good things you are telling us will come to pass, for we want it so."

December 1953, Dompago

Last July I began a reading and writing class for the boys and young men of the little mud church. Four nights a week we held school. The students used their knees for tables. The teacher [Roland] was shaky in the language, but a great spirit of enthusiasm bore us along. Now, after four months, they are reading their own language.

A new interest in the gospel has begun to stir among the young men. They began coming in twos and threes, wanting to know how to become Christians. This new interest continued until there were some 19 new converts.

However, each year there is a great pagan celebration in honor of the young men. They must take part in certain dances. They drink, slash one another, and offer sacrifices to their family fetishes. It is a tremendously binding tradition.

Of course the believers were forbidden to take part, and they themselves agreed that a Christian could not. When this news reached the ears of the village parents a great roar of protest began. If the Christian young men were not going to dance, they could no longer live at home.

Many of our young men broke under the pressure. It was a terrific blow to the church, and a big joke to the villagers. At the meeting that evening, the few who came sat hushed and limp, like Sunday afternoon visitors to a cemetery.

But what was a stumbling block to some was a step ahead for others. There was a handful who did stand firm. Such bold faith is bound to set the power of God free. It is a serious business preaching a gospel that creates issues so great.

February 1954, Dompago

We have begun a four-week Bible study course, with eight young men. We begin about 7:30 in the morning, have two hours of Bible, a little break to roast yams, a spell of Scripture memorization, some Bible geography and notes. In the afternoon we have another hour of Bible, learn hymns, review lessons, and a little French. Most of them know how to write Dompago now, and can copy notes in their own books.

I have taught them with a goal in mind — that when they have their own Gospels, they will be able to read and search out for themselves the things that are there, and explain to others. I really don't see any other way to win these people. I have gone to some villages for months on end and have not seen anything accomplished. They can't seem to see past our color difference. But if I could have one person who loves the Lord and knows His Word, and who will go and live among them, go to the fields throughout the day as they do, and then gather them together. . . .

November 1954, Dompago

Last night I had a visit from one of the young men of the church here, a tall slight fellow who has taken the good name of Bartholomew. He is one of those who took the Bible course with me last February. He has been going regularly to a village south of here to hold Sunday morning services. Two weeks ago they persuaded him to come Saturday evening and teach them the Word of God that night as well.

This weekend he found his little flock waiting for him and among them an aging Muslim who has professed to have burned all his bridges in order to follow Jesus. There is his wife, another old man whose dark business has been to bury the pagan dead, his wife, and some children. This week two new inquirers joined their numbers.

Bartholomew taught them about the new birth. He reads slowly but very clearly and people listen with remarkable attention.

They took up a collection, their second, amounting to 11 francs (about six cents). They talked about building a prayer hut. Some folks nearby want them to build halfway between the two villages, so they can join them.

As Bartholomew walked away I couldn't help but thank God for the fellow. I wish I had 50 like him.

December 1954, Dompago

I am writing to mention something of my hopes for beginning a little Bible school here.

The Lord has given some real encouragements since we opened this station two and a half years ago. By the beginning of the second year we had a night class going with about 25 boys and men attending. Then we had the one-month Bible study course [February].

As a result, new life came into the whole church group here. Many began to see for the first time that the Word of God contained a great personal message for them.

We organized a Sunday school with the young men who had taken the course and each took a group of children to teach.

By August, I finished a primer and we mimeographed 250 copies. It is giving a great boost to the work. Many who learned in the first class are now teaching others.

Now there are little groups of believers in three villages besides this one. I have reduced the language to writing and we have the first translation of Mark's Gospel mimeographed and ready.

The work is growing steadily and making demands of time and labor that one person can hardly meet. Any young person who is not too upset by poor food and long hours would be supremely happy in this work.

Early March 1955, Dompago

Last Sunday a little before sunrise a well-dressed Dompago eased himself through the door of his tiny hut, made his way over to the mud church, and gave several quick blows on the gong. This was the signal to the Christians that once again the time had come to set out for the neighboring villages. It was no ugly task for them to face — they wanted to go. In their hands they held their newly-translated Gospels of Mark and in their souls they had a new urge to share the message.

The group I went with reached our village before the young men had gone out to the fields. We didn't have long to wait for a crowd to gather. We sang a few hymns, read the Scripture, then the leader stood to speak. Our Christians witness with strong feeling. At times they seem indignant that their whole tribe is sold out to fetishism. At other times they show impatience that the people do not buy up the truth at the first hearing. Occasionally they warn their hearers with a boldness that would send a white audience looking for rotten tomatoes.

The people are much more ready to listen than they were when I first came here. We pray that there may come a move spontaneously African and altogether of the Spirit of God. Deliver us from something initiated by and dependent on the foreigner.

Late March 1955, Dompago

It's about 6 p.m. and my house is dead silent. You could hardly believe that eight young men are here with their noses stuck in their Bible lessons. We began our first Bible school classes February 1. What an encouraging group of fellows they are.

They are all new converts and are having some adjustments to make. At times their attitude seems to be that they are doing me a huge favor by coming to school, therefore they should receive a lot from me. A few have brought along their old beloved idea that to do the least possible work is the most clever way to live. But they all know that the knowledge of Jesus Christ has done something good to their hearts and they want to know Him and do His will. As the Word finds a larger place in their lives, the old unworthy things will go.

I have a great desire to see these fellows come through to a place of full surrender to Christ. God forbid that they should make cautious, stingy little efforts at the Lord's will. Pray with me that they will give themselves wholeheartedly to Christ.

Late December 1955, Dompago

The Christians' knowledge of the Scriptures has increased amazingly. They have memorized large portions of Philippians, and the Ten Commandments. They have taught their own children in Sunday school the story of Joseph and the life of Moses.

They have paid for tar to cover the walls of the little mud church as protection against the rain, and have bought a pressure lantern for night classes. I gave them no financial help with any of this.

Last month we mimeographed our translation of Acts, and this week we are having special classes every morning to help the church people get acquainted with this new book. The sitting and dining rooms of my house are about filled for these classes, adults and children studying together.

We baptized seven men from the last inquirers' class, and there are some strong Christians among them. All this is very encouraging, but I feel that I am not altogether coming to grips with the spiritual need of many of these folks. Oh, how I long to be sold out to God, for their sake.

March 1956, Dompago

Beginning a work in a new village is a thrill. Nobody knows how to read or write. Nobody has the vaguest notion of the God who made him. Life has little meaning if any.

Just now we are trying to open a new work in a large village north of here. About 45 gathered under a huge mahogany tree the first Sunday, and listened to their first gospel message.

When I returned the next Sunday they saw me coming. One welcomed me, insisting that I share his roasted yam. I teach them more. When I finish, a woman raises her voice: "Why do you hurry away? Stay with us at least until the sun stands straight up (noon)."

And so it goes, visit after visit. We sit on rocks. We teach a few verses. We distribute primers and say: "Put your finger under the picture and say 'te.' " The heat seems oppressive. It is monotonous, it is drudgery, and I don't feel like I'm reliving the story of Acts. But behind all this humble work is that one great emergency, to reach these souls for Christ.

[Here came an absence of 14 months for furlough and additional linguistic study.]

July 1957, Dompago

I arrived back on a Friday evening just as the Christians were gathering for their weekly prayer meeting. I was impressed more than ever with the earnestness and vigor of their prayers.

Sunday all day I sat back like a visitor and watched how they had been managing during my absence. Periodically an elder would speak up and say: "We have started such and such a thing since you left." Everything was handled in a smooth, wonderfully capable way.

January 1958, Dompago

The elder who is in charge of the Bible school program has been proving himself very efficient. We opened classes for the season a week ago with nine students. I was anxious that the whole thing should be their vision, not just some idea of the white man.

We had finally arranged that the local church would be responsible for the whole program — selection and support of students, their supervision, the upkeep of the classroom, and so on. The elder made it clear to the students that this was their own work, and it was not to fall back on me. "If you have needs, come to us," he said. "The white man's job is to teach you, and that is all."

This has meant a great step ahead, and I can't describe the pleasure it is working with Africans who have such an attitude. If we missionaries don't teach them to do things for themselves, we are missing the boat.

I wish you could all sit in with us, we are having such blessing together. We have a new classroom, with four big windows and a verandah.

July 1958, Dompago

I have now been here a full year on my second term. I have sought to work with the church elders, not as a leader, but as a helper, because now the great need lies that way.

Some have caught a glimpse of what great things lie ahead. For some time they have felt that improvement would come from the white man, or from across the ocean, but now they see that the secret lies with themselves.

The old excuse: "We are ignorant and poor," no longer covers anything. There is nothing in their circumstances that means they must be weaklings in the Kingdom of God. They can be princes if they wish, through Christ. These are the things I keep telling them over and over again.

January 1959, Dompago

[Roland has made excellent progress in Scripture translation, working on it with his Bible school students.]

Bible school has made excellent progress during these months. We have put up a new classroom with cement floor and aluminum roof. We have also cut stencils for 1 Corinthians, 1 Peter, the Life of David, and mimeographed 200 copies of Genesis. We have translated new hymns, and carried on weekly services in four villages.

September 1959, Dompago

The goal of the Bible school is to form church leaders and evangelists who will be able to spread out from here and show the tribe what a true follower of Christ is like.

The local church is making progress, spiritually and in other ways. Their collections are divided into four equal parts — a new church building; running expenses; their extension program; and establishing churches in other villages. This way, half of their giving goes more or less directly into missionary effort.

December 1959, Dompago

The first of our Bible school graduates has gone to the village of Aliitokemte. He is being helped to the tune of $4.00 a month, part from his own village collections, the rest from the Dompago church evangelization fund. He has six persons enrolled in his inquirers class. They are building a prayer hut this dry season.

June 1960, Dompago

[Several families decided to improve their lot by moving to the outskirts of their village. This was the beginning of a movement to build Christian communities in new areas.]

The new Christian settlement built by five families from the little mud church is practically completed. They have put up bigger buildings, with larger courts, and houses well spaced for healthier living. They feel sure that their Christian testimony will be more effective this way than when they were living side by side with pagan relatives.

Some of the more enterprising young folk are eager to settle in virgin bush. The local area is very much overpopulated, and generations of over-farming has left the soil hopelessly sterile. The topic of all their conversation lately is that settling on good new land would make it possible to farm richer crops, build up their children with better food, and in general break away from the wretchedness of the old life.

February 1964, Donga

About 25 families have settled here. They wanted their young people taught Bible, and asked if I would come. We have organized it as a section of the regular Dompago Bible School.

They built me a small hut similar to their own. I asked them how much I owed them for the hut. "You do not owe us a thing," they answered.

The students have the same good spirit. Their main concern is not how they can persuade the white man to give them shirts and sunglasses, but how they can live for Jesus Christ.

August 1965, Dompago

We have about 200 baptized Dompagos now, and another 200-300 believers. There are five trained evangelists in active service, 11 more in training. There are 10 Dompago-speaking churches. The fourth and fifth farming settlements are being started. If the number of lay workers was to include all who helped with Sunday school, reading classes, translation, etc., the number would be at least 50.

August 1966, Dompago

Mothers hushed their babies and worshipers placed their Gospels on the floor between their feet. Eight men got up from the crowded mud benches and made their way to the front of the little chapel. Every Christian in the village had come to watch these eight members calmly accept the responsibility of overseeing the flock. They listened carefully to the reading of 1 Timothy 3 and then knelt on the new mud floor for the prayer of dedication.

Behind them knelt the flock, a group of believers that has grown from 80 to about 120 during the last year, a good half of them young people in their twenties and thirties.

This is the fourth village church that has seen the same type of ceremony this year. I am pleased to see how many sincere, devout men the Holy Spirit has raised up for this task.

March 1967, Timpaa

The church gong sounded out through the quiet bush,

and men and women began to gather under the big tree in the center of the settlement.

They had come as delegates from the various Dompago churches to this, the smallest of the Christian farming settlements, for their semiannual two-day conference.

All was their own doing, from start to finish. They had called the conference, arranged the program, and prepared food and lodging for all. The six speakers were all their own men.

It was an encouraging sight, as they represented a tribe whose Christians are mostly new believers, and whose churches were scarcely organized four years ago.

The delegates were there for business. They took some important steps. They considered matters one by one, prayed over them, and made their decisions. For a young tribal church these responsibilities are heavy, but it is the best way for them to become strong.

Time and again during those two days I lifted my heart in thanksgiving to God for what He has done in this tribe. It had appeared so difficult a challenge at first, in 1952.

Roland was killed in a car crash in Niger Republic in October 1974. He was 48. He had completed the translation of the New Testament and much of the Old.

The Tuareg cross

by Debbie Osborne

One afternoon, Lena Bishop and I set out to visit the zoo here in Niamey, Niger. We were caught in a torrential downpour and fled for cover into a nearby hut. A group of young boys gathered close to me by the door, staring out at the rain, while I began to sing "Jesus Loves the Little Children."

Then I remembered an illustrated tract in my bag, with a

colorful cover reading "Come and Listen." The children listened raptly; none of them had heard the gospel before. They had been asking me for a gift of money before; now I invited them to accept the Savior, who could give them the gift of eternal life!

Once the rain became a drizzle, Lena and I went to a long lean-to where craftsmen were making jewelry. I asked one jeweler if he knew the meaning of the Tuareg cross he was tooling.

"Many years ago," he answered, "the gospel was heard by the Tuareg people and they followed Jesus Christ. But we do not follow Jesus Christ now. We follow the prophet Muhammad."

"Where did Muhammad go?" I asked.

Momentarily baffled, but not to be outdone, he said: "Medina."

"Yes, Muhammad fled to Medina to save his own life, but where is he now?" I countered.

"Why, dead, of course. In the grave."

"Exactly," I said. "But where did Jesus Christ go?"

The jeweler, though puzzled, was beginning to realize my train of thought — he had heard the gospel before.

"We don't believe Jesus died on the cross," he parried. "Or rose to heaven. He was a prophet, not the Son of God."

"Ah, but who did Jesus say He was? — 'Before Abraham was, I AM.' Jesus used the same declaration as Jehovah made in the burning bush to Moses."

Kneeling in the sand, I took off my thongs and told them the story of Moses and the burning bush. By this time, many workers had stopped their work and had gathered to listen. Then a Muslim malaam (teacher) sat down beside me.

We must have made an interesting sight, as I struggled

in English and French to present the Lord Jesus, and Lena, as she stood by translating into Hausa!

"Muhammad was a good man, but he did not rise from the dead. Only Jesus Christ rose from the dead. Only Jesus Christ was born of the Holy Spirit. Only Jesus Christ could heal the blind, lame, and leprous. All of God's pleasure rests in Jesus Christ. If you accept Him, God will accept you."

I stressed how Christ was the fulfillment of Old Testament prophecy. "A virgin shall conceive and bring forth a son . . . Emmanuel, God with us . . . he shall save his people from their sin. . . the Lamb of God. . . as the serpent was lifted up in the wilderness. . . . "

Then the Muslim malaam spoke up. "All she says is true," he said quietly. "It is written in the Koran."

When I had finished, they teased: "Are you done now?"

"Yes, I'm done," I said, almost chuckling.

The jeweler sold me the Tuareg cross for 200 francs less than what he had originally told me, and I promised him that whenever I wore it, I would remember him and pray for him."

Will you pray for him, too?

Dark Monday

by Norm Harrison

My wife, Betty, is a nurse. She knows how to look after herself. So when she came back to the house that Friday noon feeling feverish and having chills, I didn't worry. She gave herself malaria treatment and went to bed, and we both figured she'd be all right by morning.

Being alone at Lake Langano in central Ethiopia didn't bother us, either. We liked it there, looking after the SIM conference and youth camp. It was 10 miles by dirt track from the main road, and another 150 miles to Addis Ababa, where our children were in boarding school, but we had a vehicle and a two-way radio, and didn't really feel isolated. Saturday came and went but Betty didn't feel any better. On Sunday she began to feel worse. By Monday morning she was pretty sick. I made radio contact with our doctor at the SIM hospital at Soddo, about 150 miles south, and he said that I should bring her in right away.

How was I to do that? She felt so sick, and the road was so rough. The trip would take hours. But we didn't really have a choice, so I rigged up a lawn chair in the back of the van, and weighted it down with sand bags. It took seven long dusty hours to reach Soddo, but Betty arrived seeming no worse for it.

I stayed with her for the night, and the next morning decided to return to Langano. Betty was in good hands, and I had a lot of preparation to do for a conference that was beginning in a few days. She seemed reasonably well when I left, responsive and carrying on normal conversation, but it turned out later that already she had begun to slip.

Back at Langano, the radio reports I received seemed somewhat encouraging. On Friday, however, the news indicated trouble. Friday night I was advised that I should come. She was slipping badly. By the time I reached her she was in a coma. She did not know me.

Sunday morning Dr. Bowers put out a special request over the SIM-wide radio hookup. Betty was critically ill. Would the Mission family please unite in prayer for her?

I went into town to the small telephone exchange, in hope of placing an overseas call to my folks in British Columbia, Canada. Four hours later I had to return to the hospital, unsuccessful.

What happened, however, was that the Lord laid it on the heart of fellow SIMer Waldi Krahn in Addis Ababa to try from there. He got through to our pastor, who shared the news not only with our families but with the church congregation. I am still absolutely overwhelmed at the outpouring of love and concern in prayer that was manifested by our fellow missionaries and friends at home.

Monday morning was the darkest hour I have ever spent in my life. I was treading the deep valley of the shadow of death. Everything that could be done medically had been done. A special flight had been made by Mission Aviation Fellowship to bring medicine; the doctor and nurses had not spared themselves in loving care; SIM headquarters staff had practically moved the earth to make arrangements to fly Betty to England for emergency treatment as soon as she could be moved.

All we could do now was to pour out our hearts to God. This dark hour became an hour of deep testing. Was I willing for God to take from me the one I so dearly loved? It was at this point that God ministered to my torn heart with the Twenty-third Psalm: "Yea, though I walk through the valley of the shadow of death, I will fear no evil: for thou art with me; thy rod and thy staff they comfort me."

God gave me no assurance that He would miraculously pluck me up out of the valley, but rather that with the instruments of His care and direction He would guide me up through the valley floor, to higher ground. No one expected Betty to continue with us much longer. My crushed heart had said good-by. Now my concern was the children in Addis Ababa. I felt I must go to them. On the way up I stopped at Langano and with the help of other missionaries worked all night arranging our goods and finalizing my business. The hymn ringing through my heart was: "Does Jesus Care?" The refrain came back over and over: "Oh, yes, He cares, I know He cares."

When I reached the children I was once again very conscious of God's sustaining presence. Our friends, the Colemans, had taken them out of school and graciously befriended them. God had been doing a deep work in their little hearts as well. They, too, had come to the point of surrender of their mother to the will of God.

It was then, while we were bathed in tears, that the phone rang. It was long distance, from Soddo. Dr. Bowers was on the line. His message was that Betty had made a verbal response and was coming out of the coma. I was too stunned to answer.

Betty's return has been a cause for tremendous

thanksgiving. Looking back, I wonder if it wasn't at the point of my surrender that dark Monday morning that God, as it were, restrained the hand of death and began to restore her. Dr. Bowers says he can explain her recovery spiritually, but not medically.

It was prayer that upheld him in the decisions he was called upon to make. It was prayer that sustained me. It was prayer that strengthened the children. It was prayer that brought Betty through, bright and happy, and with no adverse mental effects.

Her illness, however, brought on complications that made it necessary for us to return to Canada, for continuing specialized treatment.

It is a temptation to ask: "Why does God allow such things to happen?" but we refrain. His ways are far above ours. As His children we can fully trust Him. He is sovereign.

Russ Ricketts lends a hand

"Hey, cobber, lend a hand!"

Russ Ricketts had often heard that call when he was working on construction jobs back home in Australia. A husky, good-natured fellow, he wasn't called "cobber" for nothing. He really *was* a good partner, always ready to help.

Now, on the hot, dry plains of Bale province in Ethiopia, he was lending a hand to people who were in need of the most precious of all commodities — water. For six months, Russ and his team of community development workers had been locating sites, digging wells, lining them with concrete, capping them, and fitting them with hand pumps.

It was hard work in a hard place, but Russ was well

prepared for it. Inspired by a family that had more than its share of engineers, even as a child Russ had pestered his father for tools and nails and lumber so he could build rafts and stilts and other boyhood essentials.

After studying at a technical college, he had joined the staff of an engineering and research institute, and spent months of rugged living in Australia's Blue Mountains. Following the cyclone that devastated the city of Darwin on Christmas Day, 1974, he joined relief workers in the massive task of reconstruction.

God was preparing Russ in other ways, too. SIM missionaries Bob and Joy Jarman, who worked in Ethiopia, were instrumental in leading Russ and his mother to Christ. Through the Jarmans, Russ became interested in Ethiopia. In 1976 he went out to help operate a well-drilling rig in the north, as part of SIM's post-famine water development program.

After six months there, he set up a workshop in Addis Ababa, which made hand pumps, windlasses, water tanks, towers, a brick-making machine, a solar heating plant, and a biogas plant. The 300 pumps they turned out were of two designs: the Boswell pump, designed by SIM missionary Bruce Boswell, for use on deep wells; and the Russell pump, designed by Russ, for use on shallow wells.

Then came the Bale well project, a one-year program in the south central part of Ethiopia, where families from the drought-prone areas are being settled on communal farms. The project was undertaken by the Community Development arm of the Word of Life churches, the church body that has come into existence through SIM ministry in Ethiopia. Like others on the team, Russ was a missionary in work clothes, helping people physically as well as spiritually.

The job sheet was simple: "Disease is prevalent due to lack of clean water. Provide potable water by digging shallow wells, capping springs, and catching surface water."

The assignment carried a double reward. There was the appreciation of the people when clean, pure water gushed from the long spout of the pump on a new well, and the joy of seeing them listen to the gospel. Over 90 percent of the people in the area are Muslims; they were duly impressed that Christians would go to all that work to help them.

Russ had seen that happen in other places, too, not only in the north among similarly resistant people, but in the south, among animists who worship the spirits and revere rocks and trees as the dwelling places of ancestral spirits.

In particular, Russ thought of Maazey River in the southwest, a settlement engineered by SIM and Word of Life churches for families who wanted to leave the unproductive hills and make a new life in the fertile valley. The last time Russ had been in to Maazey River, about 100 families had settled, most of them Christians, largely due to the combination of practical concern and the clear presentation of the gospel.

Russ had had some exciting trips when he was setting up a grinding mill in Maazey. Once, when driving a heavily loaded truck up a steep mountain road, the transmission gave out. Russ hit the brakes, to find that they, too, had failed. As the truck started backward down the hill, Russ made his Ethiopian companions bail out, and then crashed the vehicle to a stop against the mountain wall.

They made their way back to the SIM base at Soddo, where they borrowed a tractor and trailer, and several days later trundled into Maazey with their load.

It had been almost as difficult to get out. Some of the

settlers insisted that Russ get a bulldozer and dig a water diversion channel to protect their houses from the rain water that poured off the hills. There was no way that Russ could oblige, but they held him hostage until another solution was worked out.

On another occasion he had nursed a tractor and trailer over tortuous mountain roads beyond Maazey to deliver a load of fingerlings to a newly completed fish pond — another aspect of community development that is helping meet the need for better diet. To his dismay, the team was challenged by local authorities, who argued while the heat did its work on the tiny fish. Only by dint of great persuasion was the team finally allowed to deposit the fish and then beat a hasty retreat.

Maazey River, Bale, the north . . . those are memories for Russ, who is home again in Australia. Whatever the future may hold, Russ Ricketts, good cobber that he is, is ready to lend a hand wherever God directs him.

The night they prayed for me

by Gladys Huyler

It was in 1944, and my country was at war. I didn't really belong at home any longer. Two sailing dates had been set and changed. I had been farewelled by my friends and now my presence was so temporary that I just looked on as though from a distance. To friends in several places, it was an accepted fact that I was two or three days out at sea. I wondered how it would be to tiptoe into their meeting unnoticed, and leave again before they were dismissed?

I donned rubbers and raincoat and walked out into the streets to enjoy a last touch of rain falling on New York pavements. It was strange to be leaving all this for some isolated spot in the middle of Africa.

Down into the subway I went. I reached for a strap. For years I had done this twice a day. Now for several years there wouldn't even be a newspaper, like the one I read from, held in my other hand.

"Good News on All Fronts," read the headlines. "Little do they know," I thought. Where I was headed we were bringing "good news" for the first time. The editor's "good news" was limited to time. Mine related to eternity.

On the street it was still wet and cool, typical of October nights in New York. I dug my hands into my pockets and turned toward the church.

It had been a supper meeting. Supper was over and the group had gathered for prayer and Bible study. I squeezed into a place in the back row and listened to them sing. I didn't sing because I wasn't really there. I was three days out at sea. I just looked at them and thought: It's good that there are places in the world like this, where Christians meet. What privilege, to have all this, when there are "other sheep" unreached, unshepherded. . . . The singing stopped and the group was called to prayer.

Not knowing I was there, someone rose and prayed for me. What a remembrance to take away! What a tie to bind us together when the miles stretched to thousands.

I wanted to slip out with the memory singing in my thoughts, but I couldn't do it. I had to shake their hands again and thank them for their prayers.

As I write this in Africa on a hot, weary, ordinary day, joy fills my heart. The tie that binds me to my friends is strong and real. Because on rainy nights or clear, tucked away in the basement of that church, they pray for me.

C. J. Guth

The "utterly mean one"

by Carol Lee Blaschke

I was putting four-year-old Beti and two-year-old Stephen to bed in our mission house in the bush when the clapping of hands at the door announced a visitor. My husband, Bob, answered.

"It's Ba!" he called. "He says Nyo has delivered a baby that landed on its stomach."

My heart sank. According to the tradition of the Boko people here in Benin, such a child would be left under a calabash to die. It was an ancient custom, almost impossible to eradicate. Ba was a new Christian — one of the very few in Bokoland — and did not want this child to die. Nyo was his niece.

"Can you go?" I asked. I was feeling very unwell, due to my own pregnancy and a hard day at the clinic and with the children.

As the door closed behind Bob, I could picture Nyo in the sooty darkness of her hut, kneeling in Boko fashion, the baby lying face down on the dirt floor. Old grannies would be sitting around, whispering, frightened by the implications of this child born on its stomach instead of its back.

The questions would pass from one to the other. What

had they failed to do? Why are the spirits so displeased? Why have they sent an "utterly mean one" to us? The child must die. If it lives, it will eat the souls of other children.

I had helped many times with difficult or taboo deliveries. The problem was always present as to where to draw the line in accepting their maternity practices. Not everything they did was bad, by any means. In modern hospitals a newborn's throat is cleared with a suction tube. Boko midwives do it very effectively with a finger coated in soap and pushed down the throat.

I had seen doctors put a newborn baby in warm water, then cold, to stimulate breathing. Boko midwives dipped the newborn in and out of hot water — too hot for my hand — while scrubbing it like a pot with a wad of coarse fibers. At every birth I attended I had to remind myself that Boko babies *did* survive these routines!

Apart from the medical aspect, though, there was the spiritual side. Often I had let the medicine man continue his incantations and smoke-blowing as I waited for a baby to be born. They weren't Christians, I reasoned, and perhaps it would make them more frightened if I refused. Near the mother would be the twin fetish, a stick with a mouth cut in it, clothed with cowry shells.

Bob wasn't gone long. "They won't let me in," he reported. "She's having twins. They want you to come."

I would go, of course, but my thoughts raced on. Why was I there if it wasn't to demonstrate Christ's power to free them from the evil powers and customs that surrounded them? I had seen the fear that controlled their lives. They were happy at times, of course, as they sang and danced, courted and married. But fear was always near. Fear of the spirits of the dead. Fear of evil medicine. Fear when a child's top teeth came in before the lower ones. Fear of an "utterly mean one." Fear so strong it made a mother and father destroy their child, or give it away to be a slave.

The thought persisted that this was the time for me to take a stand. I would declare that Christ's help was greater than that of the medicine man and Boko fetishes.

"O God," Bob prayed, "give Carol strength and wisdom, and use this situation to your honor."

When I arrived at Nyo's house, things were just as I had pictured. The baby, a girl, was lying on the ground, cord uncut. The old grannies were sitting around, afraid to touch her. I picked her up and began giving orders.

"Bring a new razor blade! Where's the string? Bring some hot water! Two of you help, the rest leave!"

They sat as though paralyzed. Then old Nagui spoke up. Nagui was not a Christian, but she lived in the compound of one of the believers. She was a midwife, and, as the oldest one present, her word was law.

"I have helped Madam before," she said. "Do as she tells you."

I could have hugged her.

I cut the cord and laid the baby on the bed, wrapped in a towel. We decided Nyo should walk, to induce labor again. "Come on," I smiled, helping her to her feet. "You're not done yet!"

We left the hut and started slowly toward the bathing area, which is also a Boko delivery room. Some of the old women began chanting, calling on the spirits to help.

"Don't you do that!" I commanded. "This time we are calling on Jesus to help!" There was a puzzled hush, then Nagui called out, "Yes! This is a Jesus affair!"

When we reached the bathing area, the second child, also a girl, arrived so suddenly that I literally caught her. I wrapped her in a towel, and started back to the hut with her. Then I realized that Nyo was giving birth again!

Triplets! Triplets were not unknown among the Bokos, but none had survived birth. If only *these* could live!

I ran as best I could and put the second baby on the bed beside her sister, then back to Nyo, who promptly delivered a boy child before sinking, exhausted, to the muddy ground.

By this time the hut was crowded. I struggled in with the third child to find that some young girls had unwrapped the sisters and were placing them in a calabash.

"Put them back!" I ordered.

"We always take twins around town in a calabash," they replied "We want everyone to see them!"

"I know. But this time it is a Jesus affair. We want the babies to live. We won't take them around town yet."

Nagui came to my rescue once again and cleared the hut. I rewrapped the little ones and laid them on a mat outside the door so all could see them.

People streamed in from all over the village, and the drummers began to drum the song of twins. It was a very exciting moment.

Then the clapping and chanting and drumming took on a different quality. I saw three women begin swaying in a trance-like state.

"The spirits of the twins are coming to sit on the heads of those women," Nagui announced.

I could feel the ground beginning to vibrate to the rhythmic beating of feet. I had to do something before they were all caught up in the frenzy. "These babies belong to Jesus!" I shouted above the din. "I will not let you call on the spirits around them!"

Then I picked up the three little ones and started home. No one stopped me.

A while later the drumming ceased and Ba reappeared.

The government nurse was looking for the babies, he said, to take them to her dispensary. The dispensary, however, had been built right next to the ancient burial grounds for victims of unusual deaths, such as suicide. The people refused. "They will all die there," they said.

The dispensary was certainly the best place for them, though, and dear old Nagui used her influence to persuade the villagers to let them go. We both went with Nyo and the precious bundles, in the nurse's car. Bob stayed to talk with the village elders and the medicine man about the fate of the "utterly mean one."

When I got back, Bob greeted me with good news. "They've decided that the good fortune of the multiple birth has annulled the curse of the 'mean one,' " he said. "They will let Nyo keep all three babies."

I was exhausted, but happy. God *had* helped me, and He *did* work things out for His glory. It wasn't long before Nyo and her husband came to Christ. Two years later they were the first Boko parents to send a daughter to our school for girls. Four years later, Nyo was baptized — the second woman in the Boko tribe to take that step.

The curse of the "utterly mean one" had been turned into a blessing by the power of Christ.

Ogaden incident:

"I'll be back soon"

A strange sort of half-terror, half-anguish tugged at Mary Amalia's throat as she eased the Land-Rover through the excited crowd. One part of her was acutely aware of what was happening, the other part was dazed.

She heard the guttural babble of Somali voices, pierced by grief-cries from distraught women. She saw the sandy trail slowly unwinding in front of the vehicle, and felt the sun scorching down from the pale blue sky. She was conscious of Judy sitting beside her, and Muhammad behind her, tending the bloodstained figure of Doug. She knew that their base at Bokh was an hour away, over a desolate stretch of gravel road.

The rest was a jumble of events and emotions that refused to come into focus. Less than half an hour ago, she and Judy and Doug and Muhammad had pulled into the remote little settlement of Merkan. The whole village had turned out to welcome them, as most small villages did.

Doug had been talking to the village leaders about where to set up clinic when it happened. A topnotch doctor, bachelor Doug Hill had volunteered for a three-week stint with one of SIM's famine relief teams in Ethiopia's Ogaden. Everybody liked him. He was one of the finest Christians Mary had ever met.

It was such a short time that the team had been together. Judy Fraser was a nurse — a Canadian, like Mary. Her skill and devotion and good humor had helped make the grind and emotional pressures of famine relief work more bearable.

Mary was the veteran of the team, with several years' missionary work in Somalia behind her, and front-line experience in the terrible famine that had struck northern Ethiopia.

That, coupled with her grasp of the Somali language, had made her a natural for the Ogaden. Most of the people there are Somalis, nomads or seminomads, devoted to their camels and flocks, and the staunch support of Islam.

The team treated emaciated children, fed the starving, brought the dehydrated back from the brink of death, arranged mass inoculations, and supervised essential public health programs. They traveled and camped and slugged away in the heat and dust, happy despite the hardships.

Everywhere they had gone, the people had welcomed them. And nearly all of them listened to the gospel, readily, despite their Islamic culture, because of the team's genuine demonstration of Christian concern.

Mary forced herself to think, as the Land-Rover picked up speed between the thorn trees: Today is Tuesday . . . on

Saturday Doug was going to leave to go back to Australia . . . he wanted more training. "I'll be back," were his words. "It won't be long. I'll never settle down at home knowing what needs to be done out here."

Now this, she thought, and the tears began to well. About 10 minutes out of Merkan she stopped the Land-Rover. "We should be safe here," she said to Judy. "We'd better call Bokh."

Her voice broke as she gave the message over the two-way radio. "It's Doug. They killed him. We have his body in the car."

She blurted out the story, punctuating her sentences with sobs. "We just got into Merkan. We hadn't even turned off the motor, when this man with a knife came charging at us, and there was Doug, lying on the ground, bleeding. Then the man turned on Judy and me. I didn't see what happened but somebody must have stopped him. He got away. Doug died almost immediately. There was nothing we could do."

Reassuring words crackled over the radio. "Come in as quickly as you can. We'll notify the authorities. An SIM plane will be requested from Addis Ababa. And remember, we're praying for you."

They continued their drive through the dust and sand, the terrible scene flashing through Mary's mind again and again. A village woman had taken off her shawl and placed it under Doug's head. "You came in peace," she wept. "We said peace to you. And now he is dead!"

Mary's mind came back to the present as the car began to sway. A rear wheel was loose. They stopped, found a wrench, jacked up the car, and tightened the bolts. A short distance later, Mary's heart sank again. The motor had stalled. Nothing they could do would start it. They tried to push, but to no avail. The heat was exhausting. Heartsick, they prayed: "Dear Lord, *please* make the car start."

Mary tried the starter once again. The engine kicked into life.

The remainder of the trip was the longest drive of their lives. Bokh, a barren, uninviting community guarded by Ethiopian troops, looked like paradise.

God wonderfully sustained Mary and Judy in the days that followed: the long wait for the airplane, which was held up for two full days; the flight to Addis Ababa; the funeral.

The Word of God brought comfort. "Jesus wept," Mary read in the Gospel of John, and she felt the Lord standing by her. "I, too, had a dear friend who died. I understand." Oh, the comfort of weeping in the presence of God.

Mary still doesn't understand why 26-year-old Dr. Douglas Hill died at the hand of a fanatical Muslim in the Ogaden Desert. She doesn't understand, but she trusts.

"Perhaps the Lord is going to reap a great harvest among the Somali people," she said, "and the good seed had to be planted."

Dorothy's gift to the Somalis

Dorothy Modricker opened her notebook. "All right," she said to her Somali assistant. "Let's get started. We're going to translate the Bible."

That was an exciting day, in October, 1957. SIM and the Mennonites, the only Protestant missions in Somalia, had just concluded an agreement with the British and Foreign Bible Sociey. The BFBS would publish the Bible in the Somali language if the missions would translate it. Dorothy had been chosen to head up the project.

The task was unique, not only because the Word of God had not been translated into Somali, but because the language had no official script. There was an ancient Osmanian script, but it was overshadowed by Arabic and Roman scripts. One of the biggest decisions that Somalia had to make as it prepared for political independence was the choice of an official script for its national language.

Dorothy and her team, of course, had to make that choice before they could start work. They chose the Roman script, and designed a phonetic system for spelling and pronunciation. Roman was well known, and what little material had been put into Somali in the past had been done in Roman.

They had another major decision to make. What should be the very first portion of Scripture to put into the hands of staunch Muslims who had resisted Christianity for centuries?

Mark's Gospel is often chosen as the first portion because it is concise. But the very first sentence declares Jesus Christ to be the Son of God, a statement guaranteed to turn a Muslim off. So the team chose Luke.

Dorothy's Somali informant was a keen student of English, but he was not a Christian. At that time there were no known Christians in Somalia. The country had been opened to Protestant missions just three years before, and that only because the UN charter under which the nation was preparing for political independence called for religious freedom.

Dorothy was well equipped for her job. She and her husband, Warren, had worked among Somalis for 24 years in nearby Aden, Arabia. When Somalia opened in 1954, they led SIM's advance there. They were both proficient in Somali, and knew Arabic also.

Right from the start, Dorothy put the onus on her Somali informant to supply the meaning of each sentence. No matter how astute a Westerner may be, she knew, Somali thought patterns could come best from a Somali.

So she made her informant give her his understanding of each sentence first, then she checked it with Greek and various translations. Warren was often called in for advice. When the first five chapters were done, she started field testing.

She mimeographed them and sent them for checking to Mennonite and SIM consultants and their informants throughout the Somali-speaking area, which spills over into Ethiopia and Kenya.

"Somali doesn't have different dialects," Dorothy explained, "but there are preferences of vocabulary in certain areas."

The process was frustratingly slow, because communications were so poor. Sometimes it took months to get a passage field tested, corrected, and rechecked.

When Luke was done, she started on the other gospels. As time moved on she enlisted more Somali informants. A young man named Aden, one of the growing group of new converts, became involved. He eventually became responsible for the first draft of much of the Old Testament.

Translating the Scriptures for Muslims posed problems. One was the use of the word "wine" in the account of the wedding at Cana. Dorothy considered using the word that means "juice of the grape," because the word for wine is the same as for whiskey and all strong intoxicants, and devout Muslims will not touch alcoholic beverages.

Her informants thought that would be an obvious evasion, though, so the stronger word had to be used despite its drawbacks.

There were other problems. How could she explain the anchor in Hebrews 6:19 to desert nomads? What words are equivalent to the armor in Ephesians 6? What about Old Testament references and quotations for people who have no Old Testament?

"One day a young man asked me if Jesus had ever sinned. When I told him no, he said that my use of the word 'temptation' meant that He had. It meant to succumb, not just to be tempted. There was a different word for being tempted without giving in."

Another problem arose. The Somalis are hot-tempered people — the Irishmen of Africa, some call them — and Dorothy found that when one assistant felt that his partner's choice of words should be changed, it often caused offense. "They got so heated," she explained, "that the work stalled while relationships got back to normal. So instead of checking in committee, I had to check with each one separately."

As the months and years ticked by, the BFBS encouraged the work and helped pay informants' wages. With the New Testament nearly completed, however, the very confused political situation increased the basic uncertainty about the script. In 1967, after 10 years' work, the BFBS regretfully announced that they would not publish the Somali translation after all.

It had been assumed that following independence in 1960, the strong tide of Somali nationalism would lead to a resurgence of written Somali, and with it a decision concerning script. That had not happened. Added to this was increasing pressure against Christian missions. The future looked dark. The market for a Somali Bible seemed gone.

Dorothy and Warren and the others hung on, however. They continued their work, which by now included a good start on the Old Testament. In 1968, Dorothy approached the BFBS again, with the completed New Testament manuscript.

The BFBS agreed to experiment with Luke's Gospel, which they printed in Kenya. It was well enough received to convince them to go ahead with the New Testament after all.

But before typesetting began, a military coup rocked Somalia. Sweeping reforms were introduced, and an official script became a number one topic once again. The BFBS decided to wait for what now seemed an imminent decision.

Two years later, with the decision seemingly as far away as ever, production of 3000 copies was authorized.

They were scarcely on their way, however, when the momentous decision took place.

On the fourth anniversary of the revolution, October 21, 1972, the Somali Government announced its choice of script. Helicopters flew over the capital city dropping leaflets. The biggest education program in Somalia's history was launched, to make the nation literate as quickly as possible. The script they chose was Roman.

There were differences, though, and Dorothy knew immediately that she would have to go back over the entire New Testament and adapt the orthography (spelling and related items) to the official style. Although readable, it did not conform adequately. She began her task.

A few weeks later came the announcement that spelled the end of active missionary effort in Somalia. The government nationalized all medical and education work.

The New Testaments arrived just before the Modrickers left Somalia, however, and were put into the hands of the young Christians.

And now — the whole Bible

The Old Testament had been completely translated by the time the Modrickers left Somalia, but there were still several years of checking and revising ahead of them. It took another six years to complete that part of the work, and a few more until it was actually printed and ready for distribution.

The night the doctor changed the baby

by Gretchen Hurst

It was about 2 a.m., I guess, when Todd began to cry. Anyway, it was the middle of the night, so I thought it was the usual message — time for a bottle.

I decided to let him exercise his lungs for a couple of minutes while I warmed the milk, so instead of going to his room, which I usually do, I went to the kitchen.

Todd's cry had wakened Bud, too, but I knew he would go back to sleep. As a doctor, he had long ago learned to switch off the sound track as soon as a situation was under control. As for the other two children, well, they wouldn't hear Mt. Vesuvius erupt.

It hardly seemed possible that Todd was 10 months old already. Was it really four months since we had arrived in Liberia? Bud had volunteered to take charge of ELWA Hospital while Dr. Bob Schindler and family went on furlough, and I recalled clearly how exciting it had been to pack up and leave U.S.A.

As I prepared Todd's middle-of-the-night repast, I could still see my parents smiling bravely as they kissed their grandchildren good-by. "Who're you going to miss most?" I had teased them, "us or them?" Both our families were right behind us in everything we did, praying for us every day, and helping in every way they could.

Todd was still crying when I entered his room. To my surprise, Bud was there, leaning over the baby's crib.

"Why aren't you in bed?" I chided. "I can do this."

"I know," he replied, "but somehow I just felt I should look at him. Did you know he has a fever?"

Then he began to change Todd. I was even more surprised at that, because usually we let that wait until morning. I was about to say something when Bud looked up at me. "Hey," he said, "he's in trouble. He's got a strangulated hernia."

Bud had explained that term before. It meant that part of the intestine had escaped through the muscles of the abdominal wall and become twisted. Unless it can be reduced — worked back into the abdomen — within a short time, gangrene can develop. To prevent that, emergency surgery is often necessary.

My heart sank and rose simultaneously. What if *I* had

tried to quiet Todd? I would never have thought of looking for a hernia. What if Bud hadn't decided to change him? *He* might not have found it. But now, thanks to God's marvelous direction, we knew what the problem was and what had to be done.

Needless to say, Bud wasn't anxious to operate on his own baby. We prayed together and got busy. Bud gave him a sedative, and began to work. For three and a half hours we worked and prayed, until finally the hernia was reduced.

"We'll still have to operate," Bud told me, "but it doesn't have to be done right away. Hopefully we can find another doctor to do it."

A few hours later a ham radio contact put us in touch with a surgeon at the American Lutheran Hospital at Phoebe, 60 miles away. The following week the hernia was repaired, and in no time little Todd was walking around his crib as though nothing had happened.

That's only half the story. The other half concerns Grandpa Milner, my father, back in Cleveland, Ohio.

Several weeks before Todd's trouble, Dad had wakened up at 3 a.m. with an overwhelming concern about some of the equipment needs at ELWA. We had shared with both our families some of the hospital's needs, and both families were helping supply them.

That night Dad just couldn't get back to sleep. So in the morning he went to the office early and got his work done ahead of time. Then he started making phone calls. He stayed at it until he had rounded up a good supply of small surgical instruments such as are used on children and infants.

Through a series of God-directed happenings, he also found a Cleveland executive who was leaving for Monrovia, Liberia, in two days. This man carried the instruments with him, and personally brought them to us at the hospital.

Those were the instruments that were used on Todd just two weeks later.

That cry in the night . . . Bud getting up . . . my Dad's prayerful concern . . . the Cleveland executive . . . all of these were part of God's direction. As never before, we thank Him for the words of Proverbs 3:6 — "In all thy ways acknowledge him, and he shall direct thy paths."

The taboo breakers

by W. Harold Fuller

The chugging of a red farm tractor seemed incongruous in such a primeval setting, but it was all part of the remarkable story.

We had left Minna, Nigeria, where English-speaking African youths study Rural Science. We had left the railroad, and the thundering diesels driven by Nigerians. We had bumped our way over a tortuous trail to the SIM station at Adunnu. There we abandoned our car and headed further into the Koro tribal land on Gottfried Schalm's tractor — just the vehicle to negotiate the bush track.

Accompanying us on a rough trailer drawn by the tractor were several believers, including Adichi, the first convert from Abulu, the village we were headed for.

Ten years before, SIM's West Africa Council had approved an experiment — to open a station at Adunnu as a bridgehead for evangelizing one of the most undeveloped areas still remaining in Nigeria. It was to be on a 10-year basis. Now it was time to evaluate the assignment. What had been accomplished? Was this the right place for a mission center? Was it time to move on? Could national believers carry on the work?

Gottfried pointed ahead through the towering elephant grass. We had been approaching a forest, and now I could make out a mass of huts huddled against the trees. The gray smoke of hundreds of compound fires shrouded the thatched roofs as families prepared their evening meal.

"The Koros always build beside a forest," Gottfried explained. "They used to hide in the forest from their enemies during tribal wars."

"And now they can hide from tax collectors," grinned Adichi.

As we rumbled into the village, children ran out to greet us, blissfully unconscious of their lack of clothing. Out of two thousand inhabitants, only two children attend school — and that only at the government's insistence. The nearest school is seven miles away.

Adichi showed us his house, and the gaping hole a burglar had made in the mud walls to steal his clothes. Adichi was more concerned that the intruder also stole his precious hand-wind gramophone, on which he played gospel records in the village.

Adichi first heard the gospel from an evangelist the year Adunnu was opened. The news of the resurrection convicted him, because he knew he was not ready to meet God. It took a lot to be the first in his village to turn against pagan traditions, and when he did, one of his two wives deserted him. That solved the problem of polygamy for Adichi, but the parent of his remaining wife tried to take her away. She, too, trusted in Christ, and Abulu had its first Christian home. The young couple witnessed to others, and finally there were nine Christians in Abulu.

Nearby, Adichi pointed out the village well. The government built it to save the women a mile trip to a contaminated water hole. But shortly after, lightning struck the cement well, and the villagers blamed Adichi for refusing to let the witchdoctors put fetish on his hut, as they did each year on all other huts. The witchdoctors performed special fetish over the well to appease the spirits, and then filled it in so no one could use it.

Looking into the well, we saw rubbish instead of water. Women were once again carrying their water pots from the distant water hole.

The villagers had other things against Adichi. He refused to join in their beer brewing and drinking, which has fetish significance and seems to be the chief occupation. Villagers go hungry rather than withhold their grain from the fetish beer pots. Even infants are given beer to drink. But Adichi wouldn't touch it.

He also planted his grain just when the rains began, instead of waiting until the pagan priests said the farmers could. The villagers couldn't help noticing that Adichi's crop was better than theirs, even though Adichi wouldn't work on Sundays. Some listened to him as he helped them in their fields and told about the God who loves sinners. People were not afraid to steal from Adichi's farm, because he had no fetish protecting it.

But one thing they could not forgive. Adichi rescued taboo babies. Twins are taboo among the Koro people. So is a baby that falls to the ground in certain positions when a mother gives birth, or one with a harelip. The fetish priests are called at once to do fetish to avoid further calamity. They wrap the new infant in rags and bury it alive in a shallow grave in the forest.

Whenever Adichi heard of a taboo birth, he would try to get the baby and take it to the missionaries at Adunnu.

"So now the women are afraid of me," Adichi said. "They cover their faces when I pass, because they think I have some fetish to cause them to have twins, so I could take them to the missionaries."

While Adichi was explaining these things, the believers who had accompanied him got to work witnessing. They fanned out between the groups of villagers who were lounging around drinking beer or smoking wooden pipes. They presented the gospel a dozen times before we had to climb on the tractor to return to the mission station. As we left, some women shook their heads. "We can't believe," they said. "We can't leave our fetish beer drinking."

Back at Adunnu we saw some of the taboo babies rescued by Adichi and believers in other towns. Nurse Christel Schmolke was checking on a new set of twins, tiny mites who might otherwise have been smothered in a forest.

There were 30 children in the children's home on the station. During the past 10 months, 24 had arrived. Seven others had died. There were 13 under one year of age. Two older girls helped look after the infants.

In the face of tribal taboos and threats of relatives, the believers demonstrated Christ's love by adopting the children. The Schalms had tried placing infants in Christian homes as soon as they were brought, but too many died. "We need your help," the Christians said. "You keep the babies until they are well and strong; then we'll adopt them." As pagans saw taboo babies raised by Christians without calamity befalling the families, they came to the conclusion that believers must have more powerful fetish than pagans.

It takes a lot of rice and powdered milk to feed 30 children. Schalm supplements gifts from overseas friends with produce from his 38-acre farm. The farm also gives him opportunity to introduce believers to better farming methods, fertilizers and hybrid seeds.

"Farming is most important here," Gottfried explained. "One village head told me, 'The man who doesn't farm is degenerated.' By combining instruction in farming and the Bible, we prepare these believers to live the gospel among their own people. It keeps them related to their community."

Near the simple mission house was a school run by ECWA (SIM-related churches). When we dropped in, the headmaster was leading his 131 pupils in morning Bible reading. At the mission dispensary, an SIM-trained dispenser was treating his patients — average of 80 daily.

A church conference was in full swing that weekend. After 10 years of hard work, Gottfried thrilled to see about 100 baptized converts. Another 23 were baptized that weekend. The little whitewashed church, set between the Islamic mosque and the town marketplace, was filled with believers from seven regular meeting places in the area. Also present were seven evangelists, six of whom are supported by the Christians.

Grass-roots Bible training has helped spiritual growth. In order not to wrest Christians from their farm life, Schalm holds short Bible courses — two months in the dry season and one month in the rainy season. Eight young married men are enrolled this year.

During the conference, believers stood to testify. There was Bawa, the first convert in the Kadara tribe in that area. He told how he had met a man sitting under a tree reading a gospel tract. The man turned out to be a believer from distant Chad Republic, who had come to work in the gold mines. He was also looking for spiritual treasure, and won Bawa to Christ.

That was before Adunnu mission station was opened. Up until 1958, itinerant missionaries and evangelists had only probed into the Koro and Kadara tribes. Gottfried Schalm, a new missionary from Germany, was one who was burdened by the complete spiritual darkness of the area, cut off by language and traditions from the spiritual growth in surrounding tribes. By 1958 eleven fine Kadara believers had been baptized, and SIM agreed it was time for a concerted thrust. Gottfried and his wife Christa were appointed to the project.

Gottfried, who had suffered in a prisoner of war camp during World War II, combined deep compassion with native drive to develop the work. He showed me his burden portrayed on a detailed map of the area. Within a radius of 20 miles he estimated there to be 15,000 Koro people, apart from Kadaras and Gwaris. The seven towns where regular services are held were pinpointed, plus other villages reached by evangelists. But Gottfried is concerned about the hundreds of other pinpoints, where he has seen men, women, and children who don't know even the name of Jesus.

On the map Gottfried also pointed out a town only seven miles away where the Roman Catholics have opened a maternity hospital. "If we don't reach these other towns with the gospel soon, we may not have the same opportunity in a few years," he said.

During the church conference, these new believers, just out of paganism, discussed the major hindrances to the spread of the gospel. Their list included witchcraft, beer drinking, polygamy, farming (it is hard to resist working on Sundays), sin in Christians, ignorance, dislike of anything new, and fear (the women listed this).

They also discussed practical ways in which they could overcome resistance to the gospel:

1. Help unbelievers with their farming.
2. Take sick people to the mission dispensary, or stay with them in their compounds.
3. Demonstrate that their farms are as fruitful, without working on Sundays.

4. Live among them with adopted taboo children, to prove that God's power is greater than fetish.

The testimony of one of the evangelists, given at the church conference, still rings in my ears: "Before the gospel came, we didn't know anything," he said. "Now the pagans call us poor, because we don't do fetish. But we know we have everything in Christ Jesus."

The end of the list

George Tweedale came to the end of his list while looking out over the Ganges Valley in northern India.

The list was a long one. He had formed it in his mind when he was still a teenager. He wanted to be his own master, free to do what he liked, when he liked. As soon as he finished his apprenticeship as a carpenter, he took off to explore his own vast country, Australia.

In the steamy backwaters of the northwest, he hunted crocodiles — the largest in the world. He worked with mackerel fishermen on the Great Barrier Reef. Then he went to New Zealand, where he worked as a deer culler, thinning the over-populated mountain herds. From there he went to Sweden, to work as a lumberman in a world of snow and ice and cold.

He loved it all — the rugged beauty of the outdoors, and the challenge of hard physical activity.

But the appeal began to wear thin. He began to ponder the real meaning of life. In Sweden, he was lonely for the very first time. "There I was," he recalled, "not knowing the language, not able to read anything, a complete stranger to the people I worked with. I could have died the next day and no one would have cared."

He realized that he did not really control his own destiny, despite his physical strength, his inner drive, his ability to do what he wanted to.

"I was scarcely enjoying one experience," he mused, "before I found myself longing for the next one. The things I was really looking for were never there."

He reasoned that the emptiness in his life could be filled if he could get complete mastery of his mind. He began to read about yoga and transcendental meditation, and put one more item on his list — a visit to the Indian guru who was later to influence the Beatles.

So he traveled through western Europe, to the Himalaya mountains of India, and the home of the famous teacher. "He is in Delhi," he was told, "but he will return after some days."

While he waited George observed carefully the lives of those who followed the guru, and the worship in Hindu temples. He had a sinking feeling in his chest that this was not what he was looking for.

One day, while walking to a Hindu temple, he noticed a sign, "Finnish Foreign Mission." He had met Finnish people in Sweden, and decided to inquire. To his surprise, the woman who answered the door spoke with an Australian accent!

She and her husband, the Reverend Victor Barnard, were independent Christian missionaries. They welcomed him into their home, and invited him to wait with them for the guru's return.

Every day Victor Barnard taught George the Scriptures. It was the first time in his life that George had really heard the gospel.

His contacts with the church had been few, indeed. As an infant he had been baptized into the state church. His younger brother attended Sunday school, and won a text for memory work. He kept it on his dresser, but pushed it over to George's side when his friends came to visit. When George's friends came, George pushed it back again.

On one occasion George had been lost deep in the Australian interior with a minister. George was interested to know what this man would do. He did nothing, and, knowing that George had been baptized as an infant, said nothing at all about the things of God. When they got out safely, George recalled wryly, he had burned some candles in appreciation.

But Victor Barnard's teaching was different. Day by day the Word of God did its work, until at last the truth of Jesus Christ dawned on George. Barnard encouraged him to accept Christ as his Savior.

"I need more time to think," George demurred. Barnard directed him to a mountain resort where he could be alone. A few days later, George Tweedale, at the end of his list, looked out over the Ganges Valley and surrendered his being to Jesus Christ.

From then on, life became really meaningful. He boarded a bus for Delhi, to take a ship home. On that bus he learned the first lesson of his Christian life. "I was a long way from the conductor," he remembered, "and I was tempted to get off without paying my fare. But I just couldn't. I fought my way through the crowd and paid my two cents. That was God working in my life."

Back home, George was approached by a friend of Victor Barnard's suggesting that he go to New Guinea to help build a new Christian leaders training college there, a project of the Melbourne Bible Institute.

Five months later, George stepped off a plane in New Guinea and headed into the mountains.

"I was just learning when to stand up and when to sit down in church," George recalled, "and whether it was David or Daniel in the lions' den, and there I was on the mission field."

He lived among primitive people, hardly seeing a white person from one month to the next. It was an experience that brought him into a new relationship with Christ. He learned much about prayer. When local people would not work on a road he was building, he prayed, and God sent him workmen from over 20 miles away.

He learned pidgin English, and found great satisfaction in sharing the gospel as best he could.

When that construction assignment was done, George headed back to Australia, to study at the Melbourne Bible Institute. He took an interest in all the missionary prayer fellowships, and gradually felt himself drawn to serve in Ethiopia with SIM. To confirm this leading, George spent three months in a quiet desert assignment before applying.

George went on to serve as a missionary in Ethiopia where he used his gifts in doing building work. And even today his greatest satisfaction comes from sharing the message of the text that his brother won at Sunday school: "Jesus saith unto him, I am the way, the truth, and the life; no man cometh unto the Father but by me."

Venture into Bunnaland

If he hadn't lived among the Bunnas in Ethiopia, Charlie Bonk wouldn't have believed his ears. But he had, so he did.

He got into his Land-Rover, as instructed, and headed off into the wilderness, accompanied by an interpreter. At the appointed place, a sentinel was waiting. Following the direction of his spear, Charlie eased the vehicle into a ravine, and stopped.

The tall grass parted and an old man stepped out, holding a little girl by the hand. She was six years old, and terrified. The old man gestured to her to get into the Land-Rover, but she refused, clinging to him tightly, her eyes wide with terror.

Reassuringly, the old man climbed into the back seat. Hesitantly she followed, crouching on the floor at his feet. In a sudden movement the man jumped out, and Charlie drove off with his passenger.

His heart went out to her as they sped along. She had never seen a white man before, he knew, or a vehicle, and surely she was convinced that they were instruments in her impending death.

Charlie's companion spoke gently to her in her own language. They knew her story, he told her. She need not fear. Her grandfather had not betrayed her, he explained, he had saved her.

The old man had sent a message to the Mission, secretly, asking if someone could rescue her. She had been appointed to die that day, having been considered responsible for the death of her mother, the death of her father, and the onslaught of drought.

There had been nothing secret about the decision. The girl had known what would happen to her, and when. Her only hope had been her grandfather, but he, not knowing if his plan had been accepted, had said nothing, not even as he had led her into the lonely ravine an hour ago, weak with dread.

But all was well now, Charlie's companion assured her. Like the two infants that Charlie and Marion Bonk had rescued recently, she would soon be safe in a home where she would be loved and cared for, far from Bunnaland.

Bunnas, Charlie thought as they neared the mission station. Is there anybody like them?

Few people know the animistic Bunnas as well as do Charlie and Marion Bonk, and their fellow SIMers Malcolm and Jean Hunter. The Bonks pushed deep into Ethiopia's southwest in 1967 to build the lone missionary outpost 45 miles from the Kenya border at Hammer among the Bunna tribe. Between them, the Bonks and the Hunters manned the station, witnessing the entrance of the gospel into a tribe that ranks among Africa's most primitive.

Bunna territory is a vast semiwilderness. Scrub and thorn trees cover the landscape, gashed by tortured gulleys that rage with muddy water during the rains, and shimmer in heat and dust the rest of the time.

Although the soil is fertile, the Bunnas have developed virtually no agriculture. It is not suited to their way of life.

For crops, the land must be dug and tended and watered

and guarded from birds and baboons, all of which is demanding, undesirable work in such a hot place. Also, it ties them to the land, interfering with their desire — or need — to rove.

And rove they do, from time to time, raiding and plundering other tribes. Merciless when on the hunt, they attack not only young men and warriors, but women, children, and old people, slashing them open and strewing their intestines on trees and bushes.

Tending cattle is their major occupation. Milk is the principal food, supplemented occasionally with meat, and with blood drunk directly from an opened vein in the neck of a cow. The vein is then closed and cauterized, and the animal returned to the herd.

Hides decorated with beads and shells provide clothing for the women, who also wear huge metal bracelets, permanently fastened to their bodies. These often exceed two pounds each in weight. With a full complement of eleven on each arm, eleven on each leg, and three around the neck, some women carry as much as 100 pounds of metal day and night.

Most women wear their hair in tight ringlets, drenched with red ocher. The men pride themselves on mudpack hair styles, painted and embellished with ostrich feathers.

Clothing for men is simply a cloth around the waist.

Life is hard, and only the fittest survive. Most deaths occur in infancy or early childhood, through disease, neglect, and malnutrition. Malaria is a major killer.

An unwanted or cursed child may be destroyed while in the womb by crushing its head. Others are strangled at birth, or left in the wilderness for the animals. Authorities are helpless in the face of such practices, because of the Bunnas being so inaccessible and uncommunicative. Governing them is extremely difficult, tax collecting almost impossible.

How the Bunnas are being reached with the gospel is a remarkable demonstration of teamwork between mission and church. The barriers to effective ministry by missionaries are so enormous that the only practicable answer lies with Ethiopian evangelists. That is not an easy answer, either, because of the very harsh conditions, and the inborn hostility of Bunnas toward other tribes.

In addition to winning acceptance by the Bunnas, which involves a considerable amount of courage, evangelists have to live in isolated areas, learn the language, make major adaptations in their lifestyle, find a way to get supplies of food and other essentials, and have some means of communication with the outside world.

SIM volunteered to provide most of those services if churches in Wallamo [Wolayta] and Kambatta would recruit evangelists. Hammer station is the result. Eighteen evangelists and their families settled in different Bunna areas, with Hammer as their base.

It is the function of Hammer station to maintain communication with them, and supply them with foodstuffs and other essentials regularly. Hammer is their "bank," receiving the monthly allowance funds sent by the evangelists' home churches, and making purchases on their behalf, as instructed. Hammer also maintains a boarding school for evangelists' children, and has a small clinic to provide medical care and medicines.

MAF and SIMAIR cooperate in flying, and in maintaining simple airstrips, hacked out of the bush at key locations. These are used for special flights and emergencies.

Malcolm estimates that an evangelist needs one year to learn the language, another year to really understand the people and their ways, and another to get across the basic gospel message. "After that," he says, "we can expect people to start responding."

And responding they are. Slowly, of course, and only with great travail on the part of the evangelists. In November 1973, as the work was getting nicely organized, one of the evangelists, Peter Isa, was killed (see following article). Some could not stand the physical hardship. Some succumbed to disease and had to return home. Numbers at present are down to nine, although it is hoped that this will increase again.

"Believe me," Malcolm says, "these evangelists are God's mighty men. If anybody wrestles with principalities and powers, they do."

Those who have been wrested from this stronghold of Satan now number about 60. Of these, 18 have taken a stand in baptism, and 10 of those are now at Hammer station in a newly established Bible school.

"It may be a long time before there is any kind of breakthrough here," Malcolm observes, "but the work is still in its pioneer stage. If what God has accomplished through evangelists like these in other parts of Ethiopia is any indication, however, a breakthrough is bound to come eventually."

To support his statement, Malcolm points toward the neighboring Ara and Mali tribes, traditional enemies of the Bunnas. "Look what's happening there," he says.

What's happening is that evangelists from other areas have moved into both those tribes in much the same way as they have among the Bunnas. They are making a mighty dent in the kingdom of darkness there.

They moved into the Ara area originally, using the SIM station at Bako as a base. That was before SIM was equipped with aircraft and two-way radios. The whole program moved in a lower gear, but moved inexorably. It soon spilled over among the Malis. Today there are 58 churches in the Ara tribe and 10 in the Mali. Thirty-five students are studying at the Bible school at the SIM Bako station, and 20 Mali and Ara evangelists are in the field — some of them among the Bunnas.

This fact in itself is a miracle. The Aras in particular have always been "sitting ducks," Malcolm calls them. An agricultural people, fairly peaceable, the Aras have suffered many losses at the hands of the Bunnas in human life, cattle, and crops. Although they hate them intensely, the Aras do not ordinarily initiate attacks against the Bunnas. They content themselves with vicious self-defense, and occasional forays for revenge.

The same attitude exists toward the Malis, although enmity with them is not as intense as with the Bunnas.

The example of the Wallamo evangelists who brought the gospel to the Aras impressed the early Ara believers. They soon took hold of the idea that they, too, should share this news with their neighbors. That was how the work spilled over into the Mali tribe. They decided that if someone had brought Christ to the Aras, the Aras had a responsibility to pass the news on to the Malis.

It was a momentous thing when they decided they should also approach the Bunnas. The first volunteers were truly brave men. Peter Isa was an Ara. His murder sparked a new concern for the Bunnas, and prompted two more Ara evangelists to take Peter's place.

"If there is any hope of reconciling Bunnas and Aras and Malis," observes Malcolm, "it obviously lies with the gospel. For the very first time some people from these tribes have accepted each other and are living together in peace. It is Christ in their hearts that has done it."

What the future holds for the Bunnas is God's secret, of course. The present work is only a toehold. Like most pioneer ventures, it seems precarious, constantly endangered, held together by the personal dedication of a mere handful of men and women.

And yet, despite apparent frailty, it has its peculiar strength. Like the gossamer threads of a spider's web, whose delicacy belies their strength, so the work of the Spirit grows in Bunnaland. One small success here, one achievement there, a new believer here, an inquirer there . . . day by day the design of the Creator is being worked out.

As for the Bonks, and the Hunters, and the evangelists, and all who play such important parts in this new advance, their request is unanimous: "Pray! Pray that in God's good time, the Bunnas of southwest Ethiopia will indeed stretch out their hands to God, as so many have done in other parts of this land."

Following the revolution in 1974, it was necessary to withdraw missionaries from most of the mission stations in the interior, including Hammer and Bako. However, the work continues in these remote areas, but without the aid of radios, planes, and other conveniences.

The Bunna who "came back from the dead"

(For background, see preceding article.)

The slaying of Ara evangelist Peter Isa by the Bunnas in 1973 was a tragic blow. How God worked that out for good is an incredible story. It began 17 years ago, before there was any attempt at all to reach the Bunnas with the gospel.

At that time, a Bunna man named Gursho was arrested for slaying other tribesmen. One of the few who are caught, he was taken many miles away to Chencha, then the provincial capital, where he was sentenced to 16 years in prison.

His home village heard nothing of this, and assumed that he had been hanged.

While in prison, he was led to the Lord by local Christians. He became a radiant new man. His spiritual growth was rapid. He learned Amharic, and learned to read, so he could study the Bible. He led other prisoners to Christ, and started a "church" in jail.

The death of Peter Isa, not far from Gursho's home village, occurred about one year before Gursho's sentence was up.

When Gursho was released, his first thoughts were of his home. He contacted SIM missionaries at Chencha, and through them made his way to Hammer, where he told his story to Malcolm and Jean Hunter.

With their aid, a few days later he was back in his village, where his incredulous old mother and neighbors received him back as one from the dead. His fame spread like wildfire. Educated, speaking Amharic, decently clothed — his influence was instantaneous.

Not long ago, Gursho and his family moved into a thatched dwelling right beside that of Mahay, an evangelist from Wallamo. Today, only a few yards from where he used to live as a Bunna raider, and not many miles from where Peter Isa lies buried, Gursho and Mahay together proclaim the gospel of Jesus Christ to Bunnas, who listen respectfully and come regularly to hear more.

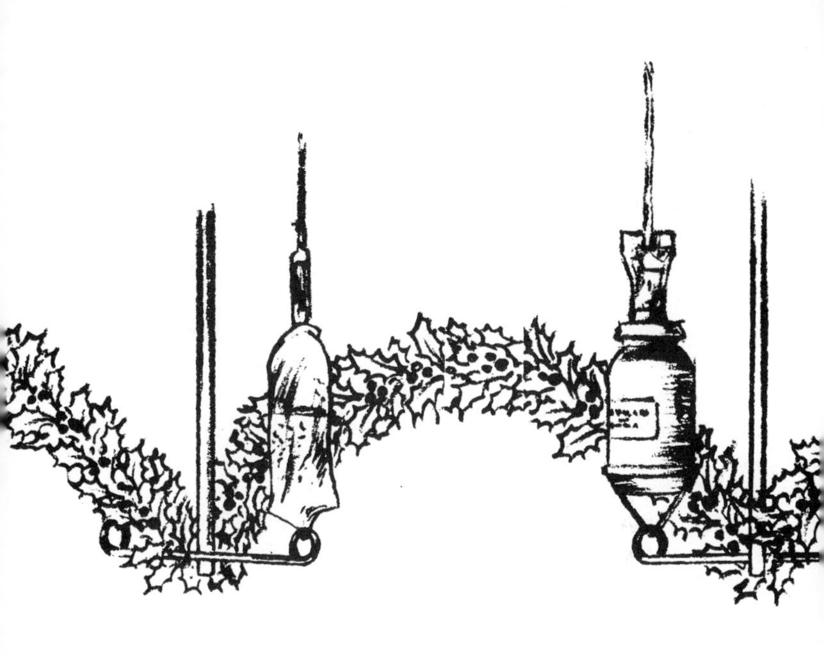

Shari's Christmas

Five days before Christmas, 1978. In the government hospital at Niamey, Niger Republic, nurse Eveline Vuilleumier checks her patient once again.

"Shari's face is very swollen. Her left leg is in a cast. She has an enormous hematoma [blood-filled swelling] on the left side of the abdomen. Blood pressure is not good. I don't like her pulse. It's too fast. She has had two pints of blood but needs more. Her hands, legs, and chest are tied to the bed. She is restless, but if she moves, her broken pelvis bones can damage blood vessels."

Eveline's notes tell only part of the story. Shari Kanengieter also has a shattered knee, a lacerated forehead, broken facial bones, a torn upper lip, and a tongue cut nearly through.

The heat is oppressive. It doesn't seem like Christmas up here on the edge of the Sahara. Eveline looks at her watch. It is eight hours since the phone call told them about the accident.

Shari, a short-term missionary with SIM, had been riding her motor scooter to the office. She swung out to pass a parked car. A taxi coming from the other direction did the same. They hit head-on. Shari flew over the taxi. Only her helmet, they said, saved her from being killed instantly. The taxi rushed her to the hospital, where a French doctor took charge.

SIM missionaries responded immediately. Shari needs constant attention, the doctor tells them, but there are no intensive care facilities and no private nurses. The hospital has no more blood. Donors are needed, quickly. Shari should be flown to Paris. A qualified medical person must accompany her.

Eveline, who is just passing through Niamey, takes up her vigil by Shari's bed. SIMers, Peace Corps workers, and students from SIM's Centre Biblique volunteer blood. Phone calls fly between Niamey, Paris, SIM's U.S.A. office, airlines, hospitals, and Shari's parents in Denver, Colorado. People gather to pray.

7:30 p.m. Shari's blood pressure starts to fall. She vomits digested blood. The hematoma looks worse. Eveline and the hospital anesthetist give more blood. Pressure stabilizes, but Eveline is still worried. The call goes out for more blood donors.

9:30 p.m. Shari vomits more old blood. Her pressure is dropping again. Eveline starts another transfusion and puts through a call for help. The hematoma looks terrible. The surgeon comes. He takes one look and orders Shari into surgery. It is 10 p.m. They transfuse the remaining blood and call for more.

Midnight. The surgeon is still working on Shari. He joins the artery that the broken pubis has severed. He drains three pints of blood from the hematoma, and fastens the fractured bone with a metal pin.

3 a.m. Thursday. Shari is out of the theater and receiving more blood . . . a total of 16 pints so far. But she is alive. Blood pressure and pulse appear to be holding steady.

At daybreak, SIM pilot Dan Germaine lifts the SIMAIR Lance skyward toward the SIM hospital at Galmi to fetch SIM medical help. At 9 a.m. Eveline goes off duty, convinced that God has worked a miracle. Shari vomits a lot but her reflexes are good and she does not need tranquilizers.

Early afternoon. Dan is back with SIM doctors Jim Ceton and Andrew Ng. More phone calls. It is decided that Jim will go with Shari. They will try for Denver, but will abort in Paris or New York if necessary. There is a flight tomorrow, but the airline cannot assure the removal of enough seats to accommodate the stretcher. Groups meet again for prayer.

Friday afternoon. The airline phones. Shari can go. Gently, she is lifted into the plane. Her intravenous bag is hooked to the overhead rack. An African introduces himself—Dr. Diakite. He heard about Shari and paved the way for her flight. He is going to Paris, too, with a leukemia patient.

1 a.m. Saturday. Jim sees Shari into the intensive care unit of the hospital in Paris. She seems OK for the onward journey. A phone call from SIM informs him that arrangements have been finalized in New York. An ambulance will meet the plane. So will Shari's parents, and her fiance, Jim Ardill.

Takeoff from Paris is uneventful. Shari seems aware of what is happening. She asks a few questions and drifts back to sleep.

The hours pass. Tomorrow is Christmas Eve, Jim muses. Time for presents. What a gift I am bringing to New York! What a joy to see Shari home, alive! Thank you, Lord, for letting us all be part of your working!

And a happy Christmas it is. Shari's road to recovery will be a long one, and a hard one, but by God's grace she will make it. Shari doesn't know it as she lies there in her hospital bed, but exactly one month before her next Christmas Eve rolls around, she will walk down the aisle to say, "I do," and become Mrs. James Ardill.

God indeed has His hand on Shari. He has on all His children.

The ring and the call

by W. Harold Fuller

Evelyn Carr blinked back her tears as she entered her room at Gull Lake Bible Conference in Michigan and closed the door. Gift boxes and packages, most of them still in their gay wrappings, were stacked in every available space. Only when her eyes rested on the wardrobe where her wedding dress hung did she finally break down.

With only a few days to go, her wedding had been postponed — again.

It was a mutual decision of Evelyn and Ray. They had prayed about it, and listened to advice — often conflicting — from family and friends. Finally they had come to the conclusion that God's answer was: "Not yet."

Evelyn sank down on the bed and recalled how it had all begun at Gull Lake seven years earlier. That was 1930, when she was 17 and still in high school. She had been on vacation with her parents at the Conference, where her father was the song director. She had met Ray Davis, a young engineering student about to enter Moody Bible Institute in the fall.

During the next year they corresponded, and the following summer, again at Gull Lake, they became engaged. Evelyn, too, began training at Moody.

In his second year at Moody, Ray was called to be a missionary. Later he felt his call centering on SIM's newly-opened field in Ethiopia. At the same time, unknown to him, the Lord had called Evelyn to the same Mission.

When the young couple heard that Dr. Rowland V. Bingham, founder and General Director of SIM, was to visit Moody, they requested an interview. It was then they received their first set-back.

Evelyn remembered her dismay when Dr. Bingham pointed out they were younger than most candidates. He suggested that Evelyn take nurses training after Moody.

But, just back from Ethiopia where he had seen the urgent need for single men to do pioneer work, Dr. Bingham was keen to send Ray to Ethiopia as soon as possible. Ray's application, however, could not be considered unless their engagement was broken, he explained, as one member of an engaged couple could not be accepted without the other.

What should they do? They could marry right away, of course, and if the Mission still thought them too young, Ray could finish the engineering course while Evelyn trained as a nurse.

As they talked and prayed about their marriage plans, they received no clear guidance to go ahead. They decided to leave the matter in God's hands — and wait. Evelyn handed back the ring. She entered training at Mt. Sinai Hospital, New York, and that fall she stood bravely at the dock and watched Ray sail for Ethiopia.

Evelyn shivered as she recalled the nightmare news that came the following year. Italy had invaded Ethiopia! Ray's letters stopped suddenly. She heard reports of chaos and lawlessness and the brutal murder of two of Ray's fellow missionaries. For nearly a year Evelyn heard nothing from

Ray. Then at last news came through. He was safe.

Evelyn graduated from Mt. Sinai Hospital in February 1937, and was accepted by SIM for Ethiopia. As a member of the Mission she could become officially engaged to Ray, and happily wore his ring again. But it was impossible for her to join him, as the Italians refused visas for Protestant missionaries to Ethiopia.

Two months later Italy decided to expel all missionaries from Ethiopia, and at the end of June, 1937, Ray arrived home. He immediately wrote to the Council for permission to marry, and the young couple went to Gull Lake with their wedding date fixed — August 10.

Now, 10 days before the wedding, a message from Dr. Bingham had shattered all their plans. On Dr. Bingham's insistence, the Council had withdrawn permission for them to marry!

Dr. Bingham explained that before marriage both partners must spend at least a year in Africa and have studied a language. He pressed Ray to accept the Council's decision and postpone the marriage for at least another eighteen months. What should they do?

Some Christian friends urged them to go ahead, insisting that their earlier decision and nearly three years of separation had earned them the right to be married.

Despite this, Ray and Evelyn decided to postpone their marriage again. Now Evelyn sat on the bed and looked at her wedding dress and recalled Ray's words: "When we can't discern the leading of the Lord clearly, the only right course is to give Him the benefit of the doubt." And she agreed.

So August 10 came and went at Gull Lake.

Five months later, in January 1938, they sailed for Nigeria, West Africa, where one year later they were married.

Looking back over many years of married life, Ray and Evelyn Davis know their early decisions were correct. Says Ray, who is now General Director Emeritus of SIM*: "By deliberately turning our backs upon what seemed to be legitimate and good, we made God responsible to work out His plan for us."

Both Ray and Evelyn Davis realize that attitudes — and some Mission rules — have changed over the years. But they also realize that the scriptural principles on which they based their own decisions still apply, and that young people who "give God the benefit of the doubt" will surely find blessing and true fulfillment.

**Dr. Davis served as General Director of SIM from 1962 to 1965.*

"The cat has rabies"

by Dr. Louis Carter

My co-worker here at Egbe, Nigeria, Dr. Peter Jackson, was bitten by a kitten one morning. It had been hanging around his house for several days, and he picked it up with an eye to adoption. But the kitten was frightened, and bit his finger. Peter thought nothing of it, until five days later when the kitten convulsed and died.

Immediately the possibility of rabies became clear.

In the middle of Africa, what do you do in the case of possible rabies? How could we get proper tests on the cat to determine if it was rabid? They probably *could* be done, somewhere, given time, but time was what we didn't have. We were already five days behind. We should have started treatment at the time of the bite.

That was Saturday. An immediate check with our hospital pharmacy revealed that our supply of rabies vaccine was finished. But at noon we would have radio contact with SIM headquarters in Jos, 300 miles north, and we were sure there would be vaccine in the SIM pharmacy there.

As we waited, I recalled a new vaccine and new human globulin mentioned in *Medical Letter,* a biweekly leaflet I had just started to receive. Unlike other vaccines, this new treatment had been 100 percent effective. Could we possibly get it for Peter?

Radio time came, but for some reason, Jos failed to come on the air. That meant no chance to get vaccine or serum by SIM plane that day.

Peter decided to go to Ilorin, 80 miles away. He would take the frozen body of the kitten to a Nigerian veterinarian for examination, then he would try to find serum or vaccine.

In Ilorin, the veterinarian concluded that because the kitten had been malnourished it could have died from any one of many diseases. It would have to go to the Vom Veterinary School, near Jos.

At the Ilorin hospital, Peter found another friend who helped him locate some serum, but there was no vaccine. The tension began to mount.

Sunday morning we managed to contact Jos. They would look for vaccine, and arrange an emergency flight. At 9:45 another radio message came. There was no vaccine available in the SIM pharmacy, but they were trying to locate some elsewhere.

What a relief it was to see the SIM plane land at Egbe later that day! The pilot took the kitten back to Jos, for delivery to the Veterinary School next morning.

Peter immediately started taking the duck embryo vaccine that Jos had supplied. It wasn't the best, and there was the possibility that it had not been properly refrigerated before SIM procured it, but it was all we had. We hoped, of course, that tests on the kitten would be negative, and the vaccine could be stopped.

At noon Monday the message came through: "Positive for Negri bodies." But it wasn't a clear transmission, and we decided to ask again on the late afternoon contact.

At 4:15 the report was confirmed. The kitten definitely had rabies.

Positive! And we were five days late beginning treatment. I reread the *Medical Letter* report: "All survivors with the new vaccine and globulin." We *had* to get that vaccine — but how? It would take another five days or more to have it flown from London.

There was only one solution. We had to send Peter to the vaccine.

He left next day, Tuesday, and was in London Wednesday morning. Forty-eight hours after we had received the positive report on the kitten, Peter had begun a course of treatment, using the new human globulin and the new vaccine.

It worked. Three weeks later Peter was back at Egbe.

I am still amazed at how God worked out all the details, beginning months before when I felt I should subscribe to *Medical Letter*, and a friend at home helped by paying for the subscription. Without that, we probably would never have known about the new treatment, and Peter Jackson may have died.

We are so grateful for all who prayed for Peter, and for all who continue to pray daily that God will direct us as we serve Him here. He *does* guide us, and we praise Him for it.

Underground agent

The air-raid sirens moaned the All Clear over Brussels as the Allied bombers droned off into the distance. At the hospital, Jo Stevens ran down the front steps, flinging a coat over her nurses uniform. "No time to change," she called to the German guards at the gate. "I'll miss my train."

Hurrying through the streets, she reached the railway station just as the train gave its warning whistle. Quickly, Jo scanned the platform. Had she missed him? No, there he was, by the clock. Jo identified him by the three small pins in his lapel: red, yellow, and black — Belgium's national colors. Jo signaled as she boarded the train. Casually, he handed her a suitcase, then disappeared into the crowd.

Jo shoved the case onto the rack and sank into a seat. "What was in it?" she wondered. Well, it was best not to know. Just as it was best not to know the man who had given it to her. Or the one who would take it from her. It held something of importance to the Underground — that was all that mattered.

Jo was a messenger for the Underground, the resistance movement that was making things difficult for the German forces occupying Belgium. She knew her danger: Underground members were shot.

Jo leaned back and lit a cigarette. She had been smoking

two packs a day lately, and drinking too much as well. "So what?" she excused herself. "I need it. Life's tough."

As the train sped along, Jo thought about some of the tough spots. Her father had died when she was nine. Her mother and a guardian raised her. A nominal Roman Catholic, Jo went to church on special occasions, and even took communion, but inside she wasn't the least bit interested.

During her last year of high school the war broke out. Belgium fell to the Germans. Food was rationed. Fear was everywhere.

One horrible experience made it easy for Jo to hate the Germans. Her girlfriend was arrested by the Gestapo because she was a Jew. She was murdered in the gas chambers at Buchenwald camp.

After high school Jo went into nursing. When the Germans took over the hospital for military purposes, Jo helped steal everything she could, to supply the Belgian resistance movement.

Now that was over. The Germans had been suspicious for a long time, and when five British prisoners of war mysteriously escaped from the wards, they arrested two of Jo's nursing friends and ordered the hospital closed.

When the train pulled into Ghent, her hometown, Jo found her contact waiting, three small pins in his lapel. She transferred the suitcase and went home.

Jo's mother didn't know about Jo's Underground work. Nor did Jo know all about her mother. Jo wondered why she looked so thin and nervous. Later she found out: for six months Jo's mother had been risking her life by hiding three Jews from the Gestapo. She shared her meager rations with them, telling the neighbors she was thin because she was on a diet. Despite her efforts, one man was caught and gassed.

When the hospital closed, Jo found a job in a bookstore.

Romance came her way and before long she was engaged to a young man, a freedom fighter in the resistance movement. By this time (June 1944), the Allied forces had invaded Europe. Belgium's liberation was near. Jo and her fiance made plans to be married as soon as Belgium was free.

But the invasion increased sabotage and other Underground activities. A few short weeks before Allied troops marched into Brussels, Jo's fiance was trapped and shot by the Germans.

But God knew all about Jo's shattered life. In the ranks of the Allied soldiers He had placed two Canadian chaplains — men who had the answer to Jo's need.

When the chaplains learned that Jo spoke English, French, German, and Dutch, they asked her to interpret for them at church parades. Soon one of the chaplains had his friends in Canada on a prayer vigil for her conversion. Within a month, Jo was fed up with the emptiness of her life and ready to accept Christ. In response to a gospel invitation by one chaplain, she started down the aisle one evening. Part way down, she stopped. Another soldier left his seat and persuaded her to go on. Jo turned her life over to Christ.

Jo was a new person. Her smoking and drinking stopped. She bubbled with a new kind of joy. Within six months she had led her mother to the Lord. And not too soon: three weeks later, she died of cancer.

Jo badly wanted to learn more about the Bible. Her prayers were answered unexpectedly. Through the help of the chaplains, Jo found herself in Canada on the campus of Toronto Bible College almost as soon as the war ended.

The instructors at T.B.C. soon learned that this fireball with the French accent had her own opinions. She didn't hesitate to speak up, to challenge them. Jo had learned about life the hard way, and when she was around, the teachers had to be prepared to defend their statements.

During school came the desire to take Christ to people who did not know Him. She applied to a mission board. They turned her down; medically unfit. But Jo had never given up easily. Three years later, in better health, she applied to SIM. They asked her to attend their candidate school. "That was a tough experience," Jo recalls. "I had to behave myself for five full weeks!" When the council members asked her where God had called her to serve, she spread her hands. "I don't know," she said. "Anywhere I'm needed, I guess." They accepted her and sent her to Dahomey [now called Benin], West Africa.

Helping the Bariba people there gave Jo tremendous satisfaction. "At last I'm really doing something with my life," she told her friends at home.

After Dahomey, Jo was moved to missionary radio station ELWA in Liberia. She's sold on radio broadcasting. "The transistor radio is still a status symbol in Africa," she says. "People buy radios before they buy shoes! And if they have radios, we can reach them for Christ."

Thousands of people who have been reached write in to ELWA — sometimes with unusual hymn requests: "Tenderly He Walks Over Me," "Hawk the Herd of Angels Sing," and "Jesus Wants Me for a Soy Bean." The English may be poor, but Jo understands the hearts of the writers.

But then, Jo understands a lot of things. As an Underground agent, as a nurse, as a student, as a missionary — she's seen life as it really is. And she's convinced that serving Christ is the most worthwhile thing anyone can do.

"What better way is there to spend your life than helping others in their greatest need?" she asks.

One thing Jo doesn't understand, though, is why some Christian young people seem indifferent to missionary life.

"Surely they're not afraid to *do* something with their lives, are they?" she asks. "Will they really go on letting the world need Christ and not know about Him?"

"Because," she concludes, "if they do, they're not soldiers, they're actors." And if anybody can tell the difference, it's Jo Stevens.

"The town is for you!"

On a trip to inland Mandingo towns in Liberia, ELWA broadcaster Fred Stoll and Jomah Kamara were given kola nuts and chickens . . . and SIM's new outreach to these Muslim people got another welcome boost. Fred relates the highlights:

Before starting out I said: "If things go wrong it won't be due to poor planning. This is our best planned trip yet." Two months ahead of time we had written in detail to the Paramount Chief of the area; for a month ELWA had broadcast the news and told about the film showings we had planned for three major towns. Feedback gave us the impression that all was ready.

There are 17 towns in the chiefdom. So far, seven of them are officially "mine." After a welcome involving gifts of kola nuts and a chicken, they say: "The town is for you," meaning that you are invited to sleep there any time. On this trip I was looking forward to being introduced to more towns.

Alas! To start with, we couldn't get near the first town with our car. The bridge had collapsed. The only means of access was a "monkey bridge" of woven vines. Was this the only river-crossing the town of Nisibolor had? It was.

Gingerly we carried our equipment across and found our way to the house of our host.

At dusk the news hit us. The person responsible for getting oil for the town generator had not returned. So, no film showing. The town chiefs seemed rather cool, which was unusual, but we put that down to embarrassment — not only for us, but for a dozen visitors who had walked an hour and a half from another town to see the pictures.

The visitors were pleased to meet us, though, and thanked us for the Mandingo broadcasts, which they listen to. We made good use of the occasion to tape some interviews, which are very popular on our program.

Next day we were invited to two town meetings. One thing became clear: we were abundantly welcome. We were given kola nuts, chickens, and rice, and told: "The town is for you!" We had already slept there, of course, but that made it official.

The chief begged us to stay while they tried to get the generator working for that night. We agreed, and went to visit another town while we waited. The oil delegation arrived shortly after 5 p.m. — but without enough. Eventually two more quarts were rounded up, in assorted beer bottles, from a small town nearby.

Try as they would, however, the engine would not start. Our host provided large quantities of soup and rice for us while a crowd of "mechanics" and advisors sweated over the engine. At one point they had it running — until they switched on the town lights. "You never try you never know," Liberians say, so they kept trying. The wiring they came up with would have made an electrician's hair stand up. The only safety factor was that if someone were electrocuted the engine would immediately stall.

Finally, around 10 p.m. the late, late show got under way, using the freshly painted white wall of the town mosque for a screen (another first). About 200 adults, children, chiefs, and elders stayed until 1 a.m., enthralled by films on the life of Christ, and the missionary film *Peace Child*.

After breakfast, Jomah recorded more interviews, and then we pushed on to the next film show site. We were welcomed. Everyone was anxious to see the pictures. There was only one problem — no oil. Regretfully, we moved on.

Our last stop was the town of the Paramount Chief. The generator was in working order and there was adeqate fuel. However, the chief was away, and the rule is that nobody starts the generator unless he is in town. Thus ended the film tour.

On the way back we stopped in Jomah's hometown, where I kept my promise to sleep. Or try to. Children played until very late, the men talked until 1 a.m., a lost sheep bleated almost in my ear a few hours later, roosters crowed thereafter, and the Muslim prayer call went out around 4 a.m.

But it was worthwhile. I gave a young student from that town a ride. It turned out that he is a regular correspondent through the broadcasts. He and his friends have sent many questions. As we bumped along he told me that he is collecting all our answers, to put them in a book. His main problem concerns the fact that Christ was preexistent. That would mean, he said, that God was not alone in heaven, but the Koran says that God is one. How can that be? Pray for Abu. He is doing a lot of thinking.

Well, the trip didn't go according to our plans, but we believe with Paul that "what has happened to me has really served the advance of the gospel." There was lots of personal contact. SIM's outreach to the Mandingo Muslims is moving from pre-evangelism by radio to more direct witness. Pray with us for a missionary couple to live among these people, and for open conversions. So far, only Jomah, my assistant, has taken a clear-cut stand.

It may be a long, hard road, but we believe that Christ *will* build His church among the Mandingo people of Liberia.

Doctor in the desert

The operating room was hot. The doctor and nurses were soaked with sweat. Eyes glued to the figure on the table, the doctor stretched out a hand. An instrument slapped gently into the glove.

"Hold it." The doctor's voice was tense. Slowly the doctor lifted a large tumor from the patient's abdomen. "Okay, there it is. Now let's get this woman sewn up."

At last the doctor unbent from the table and began to peel off the rubber surgical gloves. "All done. Take her back."

As the nurse wheeled the woman away, the doctor moved to the window and took off mask and cap. It was 95 in the shade. In the sun it was 145. The sheet aluminum roof of the hospital crackled in the heat.

A vulture hung high in the sky — sky so blue that it hurt

the eyes. The landscape was as flat as a tabletop, and almost as bare. In the distance, wild ostriches strutted among the thorn bushes.

In the shade of the hospital, a camel was tied. It folded its knobby knees and lay down, curling its lip at the doctor.

"Same to you," thought the doctor. "If it weren't for you and the ostriches, this place would be just like Texas."

But the interior of the Somali Republic, in East Africa, was a far cry from the doctor's home in U.S.A. It was a tough place to be a missionary doctor. And it wasn't just the heat and the barren country. It was the people.

The Somalis were hot-tempered fighters. And they were Muslims. Slender, fine-featured people, they followed the prophet Muhammad, and had no use for Christianity. Many of them were nomads, living in shelters of hides, and wandering with their camels and cattle. Deeply suspicious, they made few friends, even among themselves. With foreigners, their suspicion was so strong the doctor could almost taste it.

At first they didn't take kindly to the hospital. Most people wouldn't come until everything else had failed and they were nearly dead. As for surgery — well, they had to be really desperate before they would let the white doctor cut somebody up with a knife.

That was why removing this tumor was so important. If anything happened to that woman. . . .

The Somalis often fought and killed over "blood money" — payment for the death of a relative. At another mission hospital a doctor's life had been threatened when a patient died. He found a spear quivering in the radiator of his station wagon, just as a warning. It was a long time before things cooled down.

Yes, Somali Republic was a tough place. Tough enough for a man — tougher for a woman. That's why Dr. Ader spent extra time in prayer that morning. Her first name is Jo Anne.

She had known it would be tough even before she left Texas. She knew that the Muslim men thought women inferior. But she didn't realize just *how* inferior until she arrived. How could a woman know enough to be a doctor? The men spat on the ground at the thought.

Eventually some of the young women came, in desparation. Then she began to treat some of the children. When she saved a woman who was bleeding to death, people began to change their minds. Now, after six years, she was getting somewhere. Removing this tumor was the hospital's first major surgery.

The woman *did* recover, and Jo Anne's praises were sung everywhere: "She cut an animal right out of a woman's stomach, and the woman didn't die!" It was a turning point for this doctor in the desert.

Jo Anne Ader had always been a determined person. First of all, she was determined to enjoy life. At school she played a lot of sports. She had lots of dates. When she was graduated from high school she was voted the most popular girl in her class.

She was determined to be a doctor, too. But her family just couldn't afford it, so she trained as a nurse, then worked her way through college and medical school.

She seemed happy. But deep inside she felt that her life didn't have any real meaning. Then she met some people who were true Christians, people who knew Jesus Christ as the Master of their lives. They knew what life was all about. Jo Anne made Christ her Master, too.

Then, as a Christian, she determined to serve Christ. She went to Bible college. She began looking for work that had a real challenge to it. When she applied as a missionary to

SIM, she found it. The Mission was opening a hospital in Somali Republic. She would be the doctor.

Jo Anne took to life in Somalia like a camel to the Sahara. She loved the wild, open country, with its leopards, ostriches, giraffes, and gazelles. She learned to look in her shoes for scorpions before she put them on. She tried camel's meat. It tasted like dry beef. She tried camel's milk — and nearly threw up. "Never touch the stuff," she learned to say.

But best of all, she loved the people. The men wore ankle-length skirts and had bushy hair. The women had tight braids and flashing dark eyes.

Jo Anne even learned to speak their very difficult language. "I thought I'd never learn it," she said. "When I first heard the people talking, it sounded like they were strangling."

One day at the hospital she went into the supply room and found herself face to face with a deadly spitting cobra. There was no man to help her, so she shot the snake herself.

Another day a man came for treatment. He had never been inside a hospital in his life. He read a Scripture text on the wall, then fled. The verse read: "Without the shedding of blood, there is no remission."

One time she and a nurse were driving in a lonely district. They saw figures moving among the rocks — they were being ambushed by bandits!

The leader shoved a rifle in Jo Anne's face and barked: "Get out!" Then one of the bandits recognized her. He leaped at his leader and pinned his arms behind his back. "Go!" he shouted. Leaping back into the car, they went!

Sometimes her patients refused to answer her questions about their sickness. "You're the doctor," they'd say. "You tell *me* what's wrong!"

She also had to look on, heartbroken, while relatives

took away patients who would die without further treatment. But they are Muslims. They'd shrug and say: "If God wills, he will recover. If not. . . ."

Being the only doctor at the hospital was a heavy load to carry. But Jo Anne was determined that the Somali people would hear of Christ. A few came to know Him, and she is mighty happy about that.

What made her so determined to live in the desert as a messenger of Christ? Well, first of all, she wouldn't be happy if life didn't have a real challenge to it. "Anybody can stay at home and have an easy life," she says.

But more important, she knew she was doing a job for God. "Some day I will stand before my Master," she would say. "I want to hear Him say: 'Well done, good and faithful servant.' "

SIM was compelled to withdraw all missionaries from Somalia in 1975, and Jo Anne was transferred to Ethiopia, where she worked for several years. She now lives in Australia with her husband, Bill Dennett, who serves on the SIM Australian Council. They follow very closely and prayerfully the outreach to Somalis which continues from Kenya via Scripture distribution, visitation, and radio.

Somebody prayed for my baby

by Diane Warden

I watched tensely as the doctor examined my baby, lying still and pale in the hospital crib.

"We'll try the throat this time," I heard him say. "We'll insert a tube into the jugular vein and try to get intravenous going that way. He's still pretty bad, you know."

I knew. For six of baby Keith's 16 days on earth he'd been losing body fluids faster than they could be replaced. If the dehydration process couldn't be reversed — fast — he didn't stand much of a chance.

As the doctor went about his task, I prayed that God would see fit to spare my baby. It seemed like a lot more than 16 days since he had bawled out his arrival to the same missionary doctor and nurses who worked over him now.

My mind went back over those few days. Baby Keith had signaled his intention to arrive on Tuesday morning December 12, just after my husband, Alan, had left for his duties at ELWA's service depot. Lana had gone off to ELWA Academy, our school for missionaries' children here at Radio Village, and I was dressing Kent for nursery school. I quickly got him out of the way, and checked into

ELWA Hospital. I remembered thinking: "Very handy, isn't it, having your home, your place of work, school for the kids, and the hospital all on the same compound."

Keith arrived shortly before noon, and Lana and Kent were delighted to see their new brother just a few hours later. We talked excitedly about him being our special Christmas gift, delivered a few days early. In two short days I was able to take him home.

But before Christmas day dawned, baby Keith was causing us real concern. When he was 10 days old, he began spitting up. This turned to vomiting. He began to lose weight. Then diarrhea began. No matter what we did, we couldn't get him to keep liquids down.

Two days after Christmas, the diarrhea and vomiting were so forceful we had to take him to the hospital. He was dangerously dehydrated.

They shaved off his lovely soft baby hair and inserted a needle into a vein in his scalp. Then a drip of intravenous fluid was begun, and we all hoped he would bounce back quickly.

But that didn't work. Not for long, anyway. The fluid began to infiltrate — accumulate in a swelling, instead of feeding into the vein — and although they tried their best, they couldn't get it to continue. But he *had* to have intravenous fluid.

That was when the doctor decided they would try the jugular vein. When I heard the word "jugular" I reacted instinctively. "Oh, no!" I thought.

But the doctor put my fears to rest, and it was that procedure that turned the tide for Keith. For two days he got the fluids his little body so desperately needed.

But his troubles weren't over. He was still in a weak state when they ran into difficulty keeping that vein open, too. They searched for another without success. We tried giving him sugar water by mouth, but he seemed too tired to be bothered. We wondered if he was heading into another crisis.

That was Friday, December 29, our monthly day of prayer in SIM. Needless to say, much prayer went up from our family of ELWA missionaries.

That evening Keith began to squirm. "He looks as though he might be hungry," one of the nurses said. We tried him with a bottle of diluted milk. He drank it all! Off and on all through the night he drank and slept. By morning he had downed six small bottles! We could hardly believe the change that had come over him.

He was so improved, in fact, that we took him home the same day. As we put him back in his own little bed, we did so with deep gratitude to God for the knowledge that people had been praying for us.

Some of those people were near at hand — fellow missionaries who knew our situation. Others were far away — friends at home, who had no way of knowing about our need. But we were convinced that, true to their promise, they were upholding us daily before the Throne of Grace.

It is a wonderful truth that God answers prayer regardless of personal knowledge. Many problems and crises can arise in the lives of missionaries, with no time to communicate the facts to others. Sometimes, perhaps in situations like ours, we ourselves become exhausted from anxiety, lack of sleep, and disrupted family life, and our own efforts at prayer seem feeble and ineffective. That's when we depend so much on others to bear us up.

So, if sometime you're weary in praying for your missionaries because you don't have specific requests in mind, remember, God knows — and that's all that's necessary!

Interrupted by an elephant

by Jim Spady

The southwest part of Nigeria is hot and dry. There isn't a great deal of wildlife, outside of a few monkeys and baboons. How, then, did this missionary get involved in an elephant hunt?

The day had started normally. Also, as normal, our plans were interrupted — this time by a man shouting: "There's an elephant on the road!" Three of us jumped into our car to investigate.

A couple of miles down the road, two men were pointing to some trees. Other men, including police, were already there. We ran to join them, and got our first view of the elephant. He stood very still for what seemed a long time. Then his giant ears began to fan back and forth, and he turned to walk away. Suddenly the tranquility was broken by police rifle fire. The animal broke into a run.

Other men joined us. No one was armed, except for two men who had long hunting spears. We learned that the elephant had gone astray from a forest reserve some forty miles south, and had killed a man the previous day.

An hour later we saw Jumbo again, just ahead of us. The police tried to move in closer. The beast was restless, perhaps sensing our presence. Several shots were fired. The elephant swung around. He faced us squarely. I began to retreat to the nearest tree.

With regimental precision the police lined themselves up and shot in unison. The shots took their toll. The elephant trumpeted, stumbled, and fell over. He was dead.

This would have concluded most elephant adventures. But another interruption — a knock at my door at 6 a.m. the following morning — began part two of the drama.

In the semidarkness stood a policeman. "Can you help us?" he asked. "We need transport for a man who has been shot."

As we drove along, he explained further. It was not just one man who had been injured, but five. Eight police, he said, had been assigned to guard the dead beast overnight, to keep the tusks and meat from being stolen. They took turns sleeping.

One young police officer left a bullet in the chamber of his rifle. At five a.m. he rolled on the gun, which was lying on the ground beside him with the barrel buried in the ground. When the gun went off, stones, dirt, and strips of metal from the end of the rifle flew in all directions. Three men sleeping nearby received superficial wounds; another man's elbow and upper arm were deeply cut.

Ahmed, who rolled on the rifle, had been hamstrung; strips of jagged metal had torn a three-inch gash through his leg above the ankle. His wrist had also been slashed.

We had to walk nearly two miles from the road to reach the men. Ahmed was very quiet, conscious, but in shock. His wounds were scarcely bleeding. I placed a tourniquet on his arm and covered the leg wound with a clean handkerchief. Time was important. It had been more than an hour since the accident.

Joined by the other wounded men, we picked Ahmed up and carried him back to the car. He didn't speak or groan. Just as we reached the town, he began to recover from shock and started to bleed. In a few minutes we had him at the General Hospital, where he received immediate treatment.

The next day I interrupted my schedule to go and see Ahmed. He was weak from loss of blood. Two days later a Nigerian friend and I stopped to see him again. He had had surgery and his arm was in a cast.

Ahmed was a Muslim, but he accepted a Gospel of John from us. We underlined verses and suggested he learn John 3:16. When we called a few days later, he had read John and studied the verses we had underlined.

During the weeks that followed, Ahmed read the Bible we left him. Motor ability and sensitivity in his left hand were very limited, but with real determination he exercised until he showed improvement. With no less determination he kept studying the Bible. He memorized verses, and filled a notebook with questions.

One Sunday we received permission to bring him to our home, where we presented to him the way of salvation. Ahmed heard the Word gladly, but returned to hospital still seeking the truth. During the next week he again read and studied his Bible, this time with another policeman who was also hospitalized.

No matter when I called, his Bible was open. Nurses and patients alike wondered at his interest in the Word of God. One evening he told us he had never read anything in the Bible before his accident. Now he had read every book except Jude and Revelation.

Ahmed's search for truth was rewarded. It seemed to take a long time, but at last he was gloriously saved. Since then, he continues to have a real hunger for the Word of God.

The moral of this story? Next time *your* routine is interrupted by something unusual (like an elephant?) ask the Lord to use you. Through it someone may find Jesus Christ.

An extraordinary nurse

Evelyn (Evie) Rorison says she's just an ordinary nurse. Her friends think differently.

Evie travels around northern Nigeria in a Volkswagen van, carrying her housekeeping equipment with her. She assists in a dozen or more highly specialized operations in a morning, and marks it down as routine. She understands the techniques involved in transplanting a tendon from the leg to make an eyelid close, and rerouting a muscle to reactivate a flopping foot.

As a member of an SIM Leprosy Rehabilitation Team, Evie Rorison is expert in the care and treatment of patients who have Hansen's Disease (HD) — the preferred name for leprosy.

Some people think that such work must be depressing. Not Evie. "I enjoy it," she says. "Knowing that what I can do will help somebody, and realizing that it is a ministry for the Lord . . . well . . . I really praise Him!"

Evie always wanted to be a nurse, but not until she had served with SIM for 12 years did she finally change gears and take medical training.

One of her jobs is to pave the way for Dr. E. J. Cummins when he makes a surgery circuit of HD hospitals. E. J., as everybody calls him, is an expert in HD. He is also SIM

Medical Secretary for Nigeria and Ghana, and consequently is on the road a lot.

Evie precedes him by a week or so, and prepares patients and equipment. When he arrives she helps him go through a prodigious amount of work in two or three days. "E. J. began surgery at 7:30," she says, recalling a typical morning. "With a short break for lunch he went through until 5:30. Eight of the 15 operations that day were reconstructive surgey. One man had such severe contractures in his foot that he had to walk on the tips of his toes. E. J. reconstructed the foot. When the bones fuse, the man will be able to walk on the sole of his foot again. Two women had drop foot surgery."

Drop foot is a common disability that occurs when the muscle that pulls the foot up becomes paralyzed. The foot falls forward and the toes can drag on the ground. They can become infected and ulcerated and at times there is permanent damage as a result.

If the condition is not longstanding, Evie first employs physical therapy and special medication. If that doesn't work, E. J. may operate.

"There is one muscle that almost never becomes paralyzed," Evie explains. "Normally it pulls the foot down. E. J. reroutes it to the top of the foot, so it pulls up instead."

Paralysis of facial muscles is also common. Sometimes a patient cannot close his eyes. "He can't even blink," says Evie. "The cornea dries out, and this can lead to blindness. If surgery is needed, E. J. removes a tendon from the leg, or a strip of fascia (tissue that sheathes muscles) from the thigh, and transplants it to the head. He attaches one end to the temporalis (jaw) muscle, and tunnels it around the eyelid. When the patient chews, he can close his eyes."

Muscle paralysis occurs frequently because of the nature

of HD. "Leprosy bacilli attack the skin and the nerves," Evie explains. "If the nerves that supply a muscle are damaged, that muscle becomes paralyzed."

Surgery isn't usually done unless therapy and medication fail, and the disease is inactive, so it will not continue its destructive work.

Evie often handles a scalpel herself. "I repair eyelids that have turned inward, usually a result of trachoma, and do skin grafts and biopsies. At times I incise fingers that have tendon sheath infections."

After E. J. leaves, Evie stays to give personal attention as necessary, and to instruct Nigerian attendants in specialized care. A patient may be in a cast for several weeks, or need prolonged therapy. Exposure to the gospel during this time brings good response.

"I went into the surgical ward the other day," Evie recalls, "and heard a patient quoting Scripture. He was a well-educated Muslim whom the hospital evangelist had led to Christ. The news spread quickly, and many Muslims came to talk with him."

The results of SIM ministry to HD patients over the years have been impressive. In fact, HD treatment was a major factor in opening the strongly Islamic northern section to the gospel, when Nigeria was under British rule. Every SIM HD center has a flourishing church and Bible teaching ministry.

Typical of many converts is Iro, a Muslim who came to the Sokoto center about nine years ago. He became a Christian, learned to read and write, and grew in his understanding of the Word. After five years his disease was arrested, but his left hand was deformed; he could not close it. After discharge he went to an SIM Bible school, and then became pastor of the church at Sokoto, where he had been healed and converted. E. J. has recently repaired his hand.

Evie has seen a lot of changes take place in the treatment of HD patients. "The picture simply isn't what it used to be," she explains. "Most people have a natural resistance to HD. In fact, it's considered one of the least contagious of infectious diseases. It's quite safe for most patients to live normal lives. This means that most patients don't live in leprosaria, and no babies are taken from their mothers." She says she is not afraid of contracting the disease. "I touch the patients, of course, but I take precautions."

With this change, leprosy centers in Nigeria have been converted into hospitals for special treatment only. Village clinics have been opened, where HD patients go each week for treatment and examination.

"In this way, HD is considered just another disease, not something apart. The chances of deformity are reduced, too, because the disease is diagnosed early and treatment begun."

The cause of deformity is often misunderstood, Evie says. She stresses the fact the HD does not "eat away" tissue. There is a form of HD that raises nodules on the face, and causes disfigurement that way, especially if infection sets in, but the loss of fingers or toes or noses usually is because of ulceration. HD attacks the nerves and causes anesthesia — numbness. Then comes damage through burns, insect bites, cuts, abrasions, or some other way. If infection sets in, it can go unnoticed at first because there is no feeling. Infection can lead to ulceration and loss. The gruesome pictures of patients with no hands or feet are almost always pictures of what ulceration has done, not HD itself.

The hospitals also provide special aids such as crutches and wooden legs and customized shoes for deformed feet. "We instruct patients thoroughly in the care of hands and feet," she says, "because they will always be anesthetized.

Sometimes the heads of the metatarsal bones in the foot will cause pressure, and E. J. will remove them. This makes a soft cushion to walk on. At times there are amputations, but we try to save the extremity by taking dead bone out."

Evie is based in Kano and travels almost constantly, examining patients and instructing attendants at the many village clinics, as well as at three major SIM HD hospitals. She drives 150 miles to the Maradi Leprosarium, across the border in Niger Republic; 215 miles to Bauchi; and 326 miles to Sokoto. "I traveled 1290 miles in the last 16 days," she reported recently. "Some of the roads were terrible — washboard, sand, and potholes. I examined 1245 patients, and discharged 294."

But Evie's perspective is eternal. Diseased bodies need help, and she gladly gives it, but she is even more concerned about spiritual needs. To see those needs met, through faith in Christ, is what brings Evie her greatest joy.

Not long ago she had eight patients crammed into her van as she drove them to hospital. "You can't imagine the happy time we had," she recalls. "Most of them were Christians, and they sang hymns so beautifully most of the way. It made me think how wonderful it will be in heaven! I'm so glad I'm able to help these brothers and sisters in the Lord, as well as those who have not yet trusted Him."

That's the kind of dedication that makes Evie Rorison an extraordinary nurse.

Trial and triumph

Leprosy among missionaries is extremely rare. Yet, in the wisdom of God, this missionary (whose name is purposely withheld) was allowed to taste a little of the cup of suffering which so many Africans drink.

So this was it! I was sitting alone in a hospital room in New York City when the doctors came to deliver the verdict. The laboratory test was positive — I had leprosy*. They left me and I was alone again with my thoughts.

When I had arrived home from Africa for furlough a little earlier that year (1932) one doctor had queried my condition and for some time the argument raged back and forth. "It is!" said one. "It isn't!" said another. Nothing positive could be found until that day. I had been moved from a ward to a small private room a few days before, but I had no idea of the reason. Here it was. I was left alone to face it.

Did I say alone? No, I was not alone, for my Lord was with me. Even in my solitude I had my Bible, and the strength that the Lord alone could give. Visitors from Mission headquarters were most kind, but the hospital insisted that all visitors wear special gowns and masks.

Then one of our older missionary ladies marched in through the door without all the paraphernalia, and threw her arms around me.

"May God fill you with His grace," she said. "You are one of the Lord's chosen, to suffer this affliction."

This did me more good than anything else, as she was the last person I thought of coming to me in that way.

What now? Why should I not return to Africa? Treatment was begun immediately, and as soon as possible I set out. But our Mission doctor in Africa at that time could not see how it could possibly be leprosy, and after a few months stopped the treatment. After all, I had been in Africa only three years when the first symptoms were noticed. Experts said it could not possibly have developed within that length of time. What contact had I with leprosy sufferers? None that I knew of. I knew of only one such man in the town, but I saw him only at a distance. My first contact with leprosy remains a mystery. It could even have been before coming to Africa.

When I had first come to Africa I had been sent to a school to teach. The first year I spent mainly learning the language. Then I began teaching full time.

I accepted local conditions as I found them, without any great shock. I expected them to be grim. I wanted to understand the people, their needs, their problems. I wanted to "sit where they sat." Little did I know how God would bring that about.

After three years I noticed that the feeling in one foot was not normal — that was all. I mentioned it to the doctor, who thought I was overtired, and that it would disappear as I rested. It didn't. Very, very gradually this disturbance increased in hands and feet. Nothing more.

Shortly before the scene in the New York hospital I noticed I was unable to do things that had been easy for me, but adapted myself to it by finding other ways. By the time the diagnosis was made and treatment begun, permanent damage had been done in the nerves of the hands and feet.

Now, back in Africa, the controversy continued. It would have been easier for me had the first diagnosis been accepted by all, and I could have thought it through on the spiritual level, once for all. But no, the Lord did not will it that way. I was tested to the uttermost. My hopes were raised one day, and dashed the next.

No one on the outside knew how the battle raged, except perhaps my co-worker, who stood by me through thick and thin, year after year. The Lord did not ask me to go through this all alone, but provided a staunch friend to stand beside me.

All this time I was doing regular missionary work but took necessary safeguards in contacts with others. My fellow missionaries understood, and were very gracious. Had it been possible to forget, they would have helped me to do so. If any had criticism they kept it to themselves. Some were terrified, but I only heard about it in a roundabout way. I tried not to give offence anywhere. Nevertheless there was always the fear of not being wanted, of people shunning me at any time.

Then came furlough again. My greatest trial at this time was being sent from one doctor to another, all making the same tests, all asking the same questions, but coming up with different answers.

Finally it was established that the first diagnosis in New York was correct, but that the case was considered closed.

In those days treatment of leprosy was not as developed as it is now, and I was put on a "preventative" treatment which proved my undoing. It lowered my vitality to such an extent that the leprosy became active again.

I finished my furlough and had left New York on my way back to Africa when word came that I could not return because of medical regulations. I did not know of this until I was greeted with the news when I landed in Africa. What a blow! Physical vitality was at its lowest ebb, and my hopes were dashed to the ground.

But the Lord had His hand in this, too. Our Mission doctor in Africa prescribed just the treatment I needed to build up physically and to end the activity of the disease itself. He also gave me the spiritual boost I needed.

When my colleague and I arrived back in New York we were armed with treatment and the help necesary to begin the battle back to health. This time we knew where we were going, and what to do.

Friends at home accepted our explanations without question, and the few who knew were very gracious and helpful. I knew no sense of rejection by others, but there was always that thought that some thoughtless person might start a scandal.

In some ways the following months were hardest. Physical weakness and mental depression made spiritual victory difficult, but God proved sufficient, even in this trying time.

Bit by bit strength came back, and the day finally came when I was pronounced symptom free, and we could return to our work. It did not take us long to get back to Africa, and our old tasks, praising the Lord for all He had done.

For a person who is naturally very active, even the partial loss of the use of hands and feet has proved a sore trial. When I was young I said I would rather be blind than not have the full use of my hands. Yet the Lord has permitted even that to happen to me, and still His grace is sufficient.

God brings us to the place of utter helplessness to show us His sufficiency. Some of the things I loved to do are impossible for me now, but He has opened other things to me, and caused me to place my whole confidence in Him.

Now as I see people in Africa suffering from leprosy, I can truly "sit where they sit." I know a little of what they pass through. And yet I don't, for most of them do not have the loving care of Christian friends which I had, nor do they have the internal strength of God's Holy Spirit in the darkest hour. As I see them I long that they should come to know my Savior, my Comforter.

Some years ago it was thought better to give me work that did not require so much activity and where I would not be among people so much. I felt very unfitted for this new assignment, as it did not follow my "natural abilities." But the Lord is not dependent on natural ability, even though He is the one who gave it in the first place. This new work has meant a new dependence on Him. Anything that is accomplished is all of Him.

It is my prayer that this trial which the Lord has seen fit to place upon me, and yet to carry with me, may be used of Him to help any of His children who are laboring under a heavy and prolonged trial. He has a purpose to accomplish in it all — perhaps to help another, but surely to refine me as gold, that I may be made like Him.

Because of the stigma attached to the word "leprosy," the preferred medical term today is "Hansen's Disease."

Doxology

by Suzi Klomparens

It was in May 1972 that Tim gave me my diamond. He had come to my apartment and hung some curtains for me, and we were just getting ready to go to a concert, and then all of a sudden he pulled this box out of his pocket and asked me if I would like a little present.

That was pretty exciting. After the concert we went to my folks, and then to Tim's, and everybody was very happy, including us.

I could talk for hours about our courting days. We did a lot of fun things together. We went to hockey games in the winter, and double dated with our friends, but mostly I recall times when we just shared together. Tim was the first boy I ever knew who was really interested in missions, and we found we just had so much to talk about.

I had come to Christ as a child, and was about 12 years old when a missionary from the Philippines came to our church. Seeing his concern really reached into my heart. I told the Lord I wanted to be a missionary some day, too.

Mind you, as I grew up, several times I wished I could

forget that commitment, because I was starting to think that I would rather settle down in comfortable U.S.A. But I knew what God wanted me to do, so when Tim and I met and realized we both had the same longing, it was terrific.

We were married on December 22 that year, and I worked while Tim finished college. Then he worked and put me through school. All that time we had an awareness of wanting to serve God, but we weren't drawn to any one area or kind of work.

The week before Tim graduated he was out doing visitation with a friend from the church who was heading for the mission field. He got talking about how his mission needed agricultural missionaries. Tim was very interested in agriculture, which was quite funny because he was a real city kid.

That same week he was talking with SIM leader Dr. Raymond Davis, who is a member of our church (Berean Baptist, Grand Rapids, Michigan) and who was saying how SIM was involved with agriculture and had some special personnel needs.

Well, the outcome of it all was that Tim enrolled at Michigan State University and took classes in agricultural mechanics and things like that. It was really interesting to find that the first counselor Tim had at Michigan State had worked with Wycliffe Bible Translators, and was right up on the subject of agriculture and missions.

We also kept in touch with SIM, and in due time we were being processed as candidates.

We were so happy together, especially when we were accepted as missionaries to Nigeria and saw our friends back us with promises of financial support. Equally exciting was the news that our first child was on the way after four years of marriage!

There was only one flaw. Tim began to suffer from

fatigue, and to feel constant pain. His problem intensified until exploratory surgery had to be scheduled. While we waited for that appointment, our minds whirled with frightening thoughts. The awful word "cancer" constantly surfaced. I felt, no, it couldn't be, not with the definite leading we'd had thus far.

On Sunday evening November 13, 1977, Joel Timothy joined our family. On Thursday the baby and I came home. On Friday Tim entered the hospital. I think I knew that surgery would reveal a malignancy, but I kicked myself mentally, thinking that I was showing a lack of faith. "Why would God allow that?" I asked.

My fears were confirmed. It was cancer. There was more surgery, and then radiation treatment. Tim longed to be able to enjoy his new son, but he was too ill. He kept a daily devotional diary in which he wrote his inner thoughts. Just before Christmas he wrote: "God is able to give me the right kind of attitude, one of happy, joyful submission to His will."

On December 31 it was: "What does 1978 hold? I only know that as I give it into God's hands He will work it all out for our good."

And on January 1/78: "The love Suzi and I have for each other just grows and grows through this experience. Praise the Lord for all the things He brings into our lives."

About February he began to improve and at one point he felt so well we began to resume our plans to go to Africa. Almost overnight those plans were shelved and new plans began — chemotherapy treatments. Events then transpired in rapid, traumatic succession. Everything the doctors warned could go wrong did. Tim's kidneys shut down, he lost blood, he developed pneumonia, and finally went into a coma.

Throughout the whole ordeal, though, he never complained. He told a friend: "If this is God's will for me, I don't want out of it."

Tuesday night, May 23, I shall never forget. Tim's mother and I had taken turns staying around the clock with Tim, who was on a respirator. I was overwhelmed with weariness, and my heart and mind were trying to deal with the whole matter of Tim's approaching death. In the wee hours of the morning I cried out to the Lord.

He answered through His Word. Just before dawn I read in Psalms: "When I am afraid, I will put my confidence in you. . . . You have seen me tossing and turning through the night. . . . You have collected all my tears. . . . This one thing I know, God is for me."

I must have read that half-a-dozen times. Then came the climax: "O God, my heart is quiet and confident. . . . Let us greet the dawn with song."

Across the hall I could see the sun just coming up. Quietly, yet nearly bursting with joy and peace, I sang the Doxology.

That evening God took my darling Tim Home.

Although there have been difficult times of real loneliness since then I can honestly say that although I would never have chosen this direction, I would not exchange it now for anything. It has been one of the most thrilling times of my life as I have watched the Lord lead me and my little son. He has provided for our every need, and shown Himself to truly be a "father to the fatherless and a husband to the widow."

Suzi's commitment did not end with Tim's death. A year later she left for Nigeria, with little Joel, to serve as an SIM missionary at Kent Academy, school for missionaries' children.